The
Creative Brief
BLUEPRINT

CRAFTING STRATEGY
THAT GENERATES
MORE EFFECTIVE
ADVERTISING

Kevin McTigue
Derek D. Rucker

ISBN (Print): 978-1-09839-045-7
ISBN (eBook): 978-1-09838-076-2

Contents

About the Authors

. . . .

Kevin McTigue is a clinical associate professor of marketing at Northwestern University's Kellogg School of Management teaching multiple classes for the MBA program and executive education, where he is a two-time winner of the Core Course Teaching Award. His career spans more than twenty years in teaching, consulting, brand management, and advertising. He has written or evaluated hundreds of creative briefs for everything from social media for a children's hospital to Super Bowl ads for consumer-packaged goods.

Before his full-time appointment at Kellogg, Kevin led the strategy and consulting practice in the central region of the US for global digital agency SapientRazorfish. His work focused on driving value for clients in the digital age. He advised senior Fortune 500 clients on how to best leverage digital platforms to create value, from marketing strategies to digital transformation road maps to the creation of entirely new businesses.

Prior to SapientRazorfish, he spent seven years in brand management with Tyson/Hillshire Brands/Sara Lee leading businesses including Jimmy Dean, Ball Park, and Hillshire Farm. Over this time he developed and launched multiple products, repositioned and developed new campaigns, and led all activities related to planning and running the business. Kevin spent significant time working in digital and traditional advertising at agencies such as marchFIRST, JWT, and BBDO. He also led brand strategy and campaign development for clients including Nestlé, Unilever, and Mars/Wrigley.

Dr. Derek Rucker holds the Sandy & Morton Goldman Professorship of Entrepreneurial Studies in Marketing at the Kellogg School of Management. Trained as a social psychologist, his academic research interests and pursuits focus broadly on consumer behavior with an emphasis on advertising, persuasion, social hierarchy, and compensatory consumption. He explores questions related to what makes for effective advertising and what motives underlie consumer consumption. He has contributed to more than 130 academic publications including leading journals such as the *Journal of Consumer Research*, the *Journal of Marketing Research*, the *Journal of Marketing*, and the *Journal of Consumer Psychology*. His research has been covered in major media outlets such as the *New York Times*, *Time* magazine, and ABC News.

Dr. Rucker currently teaches advertising strategy at Kellogg. The course focuses on basic psychological principles to better understand how to plan and execute successful advertising. A central aspect of his course is the writing, evaluation, and revision of creative briefs. His students have gone on to do impressive brief work for brands such as Mattel, Old Spice, Unilever, and Tyson. In recognition of his commitment to teaching excellence Dr. Rucker has won both the Sidney Levy Teaching Award and the Top Elective Professor Award. In addition to his work in the classroom, Dr. Rucker is a co-instructor of the annual Kellogg Super Bowl Advertising Review.

Acknowledgments

. . . .

Many of the ideas explored in this book are the result of our experiences with wonderful minds throughout our careers. These include our colleagues at Kellogg and our friends at brands and agencies, as well as our students. In particular, we would like to acknowledge several people who graciously gave their time in creating this book whether it be bouncing off ideas or looking at early drafts: Tim Calkins, Molly Hayes, Ian Sohn, and Mike Stratta.

We also add particular thanks to Mauricio O'Connell, Kellogg class of '08, who read the entire book from front to back. Moreover, he offered precise comments that challenged us to push our ideas a little further along each step of the journey.

We also thank Adisa Fazlovic for her help in providing the perfect amount of whimsy in the illustrations throughout the book.

Finally, we would like to thank our families—without their love and support none of these ideas would have ever moved beyond a blueprint.

Why

. . . .

You're building your dream house. It is a house you want to live in, a house you want to entertain in, a house you want to share with your friends and family. How would you build this house? Would you hire qualified builders and say, "Please build me a house. See you when it's finished," or "Do whatever you want to do; I don't care"? No—if you're at all like us, you'd make plans first. You'd make sure everyone understands the blueprint. Before you meet with a builder, you'd meet with an architect. She would ask you what you want. How many bedrooms? Are you really into cooking? Do you want a home theatre setup for your family? Do you plan to entertain for large parties or more intimate occasions? What is your budget? The architect would work to understand your goals and translate them into a clear blueprint for the builder. You would put all this work into the blueprints because, with proper thought and careful diligence, the blueprints would allow your dream home to be built to serve your specific needs within your budget. And if you are walking through the house during construction and see something amiss, you would go back to the blueprint as a basis for your discussion with the builder.

We have written this book with a similar idea in mind. Too often in practice, we see brands hand poor strategies to their agency or creative partner. Sometimes it's as bad as "Please make me an ad. Let me know when it's finished." Much like we would want a blueprint to build a house, we need a plan to develop successful executions. Throughout this book, we use the term **execution** to refer to any number of potential creative outputs such as advertisements, communications, logos, social content, and other forms of messaging. If you are creating an execution that is intended to have value and impact, then you need to start with a strategy.

For us, the blueprint for an execution manifests in the form of a **creative brief**. Like a blueprint, the creative brief is a means to offer guidance, direction, and even inspiration to advertise your product, service, or business. If you see something amiss in the creative work, you have a reference point, like a blueprint, to discuss your vision and plan with your creative partner or agency. But let's back up for a moment. What exactly is a creative brief?

A creative brief is a document developed by the client—the person for whom the advertising or communication serves—that outlines the objectives, intended target, insights about the target, the main message, important details about media or production, and expected measurement of the execution's success. The creative brief is shared with an agency or creative partner—the person or persons responsible for bringing to life the tactical execution. In some cases, the creative brief might be a cocreated document. In other cases, especially for smaller firms and entrepreneurs, the client might be the sole party responsible for the creative brief. However, regardless of the size of the team behind the creative brief, a creative brief is the strategic nucleus of a campaign. It is the blueprint that guides the building of your advertising campaign. This observation is true whether you are interested in a video advertisement, a series of social media posts, an email, a logo, or even creating an experience. A proper creative brief provides all the necessary information to guide the team to produce the desired outcome so that you get the output you want.

Through decades of combined experience, we have seen countless examples of creative briefs—or "briefs" for short—and the ensuing ad campaigns. We have also seen a wide range of successes and failures when it comes to briefs and campaigns. Brands that have consistent success in their executions have produced strong creative briefs as part of that process. Indeed, in our course on advertising strategy at Northwestern's Kellogg School of Management, we have helped numerous students and executives alike become adept at the creative brief writing process. And MBA students from our program have gone on to do amazing creative brief work for brands such as Apple, Häagen-Dazs, Amazon, Nike, Kraft-Heinz, Caterpillar, Modelo, Mattel, and Old Spice to name but a few. Many of our students have gone on to successfully launch their own brands as entrepreneurs, and they too did some great brief work! To us, writing a powerful creative brief is arguably the most important role of the client in the process of developing an execution. And it is the best way to shift the curve of your success to create consistently better communications. A great creative brief can also save a lot of time and money by focusing partners and avoiding costly restarts and churn.

Let's pause here. The reason we chose to write this book is twofold. First, we have both come to understand and appreciate that strong creative briefs can transform brands. A proper strategy laid out in the creative brief can be the difference between becoming a category leader or going bankrupt. Mastering the construction of the creative brief will allow you to achieve meaningfully better communications linked to growth and profit. Second, we have noticed that, despite its importance, proper strategic diligence in developing communications is wildly inconsistent across brands, companies, and categories. We have observed many unsuccessful campaigns that ranged from ineffective to disastrous. The proliferation of digital options has not led to systematically better and more effective results. In fact, it is leading marketers to shift their attention away from strategy toward shiny new tactics that are ineffective. We sometimes hear that digital technology allows you to test ads more easily—you can test ad A versus ad B—but A/B testing doesn't solve your problems when options A and B are both bad! Most ads aren't good. Most briefs aren't good. Let's fix that.

The brief format we use in this text draws from a myriad of examples we have seen and used over the years. Our format encapsulates the most important elements. In practice, it is quite likely that whatever version of the brief document you encounter, it will share these key elements (or it should!). For brands we admire with regard to their brief writing practices, departures from our structure more often reflect subtle taste or preference tweaks than strong differences in strategy.

In this book, following a brief introduction, we generally divide each chapter into three sections meant to accomplish distinct objectives. First, we articulate why the topic of each chapter is valuable to the client—that is, the person commissioning the advertising—and then why it is important to the agency—that is, the creative partner meant to transform the strategy into creative work. Second, we explain why brands fail and how they can succeed on issues related to the topic. In a number of our chapters, this discussion also involves examining a brief and seeing how to improve it. Third, we share myths, misconceptions, and other questions on the topic. As more questions come in, we'll answer them on our website: Creativebriefblueprint.com. In the current chapter, our emphasis is on the creative brief.

Value to Clients and Agencies

For clients—the person or brand the advertising is designed to promote— the creative brief serves two basic functions:

1) It provides an informative and ideally inspiring road map for the development team.

2) It offers an aligned set of strategic criteria to evaluate the output.

On the first function, as we discuss and illustrate throughout this book, a creative brief confronts clients with a series of questions that must be answered to develop a compelling strategy. "What are we trying to accomplish through this communication?" "Who are we talking to?" "What's the most important thing we can say?" "How will we know if this is a success?" A creative brief can help clients either affirm that due diligence has been done to answer the questions properly or reveal where ambiguity exists and must be resolved. In essence, a creative brief forces strategic thinking and rigor that dissuades clients from the temptation of simply making things up or leaving critical information out—which sadly happens all too often!

On the second function, the creative brief provides clients with a powerful means not to just inform, but to guide strategic feedback to an agency partner during development. That is, the creative brief provides a structure to share critical feedback to help you get the best out of your creative. Moreover, a creative brief holds you accountable; if you ask for the wrong thing, the creative can point out that is what you asked for. As such, a creative brief is a means to help educate clients and interact with agencies and/or the person doing the creative work to help both parties engage effectively and to achieve mutually desired results.

Agencies—which will create and produce the advertising—want to receive strong briefs from clients. Good agencies have two primary goals: make money and do great work. A strong brief facilitates both. With regard to profits, most agency compensation models are built on the time of specific people allotted to an account for a given project or time frame. A sound brief offers a clear road map for what is expected and reduces the churn or "swirl" that can accompany creative development. Churn costs money. Churn burns out resources. Churn leads to a tepid "I know they'll approve this" type of creative output. Agencies want to make great communications because that makes them famous, wins awards, brings in more clients, and fulfills their creative desires. These observations apply to whether you are working with a world-renowned agency such as Wieden + Kennedy or your own internal agency or creative partner.

For us as consumers, great executions are different and stand out. Great executions make us feel like the brand knows us. Great executions move us. Great creative briefs inspire and focus creative energies so they can move consumers and drive businesses. Agencies want such outcomes and so do you!

Of course, writing strong creative briefs takes time. Through this book, we go through the brief in detail, examining each part and providing specific context.

Where Brands Fail and How to Succeed

Why do brands fail and how can they succeed when it comes to the creative brief? One of the most glaring and unacceptable reasons brands fail is that they *never write a brief.* This happens all too often. For example, a nonprofit asked one of us to help choose a new logo for the organization because the team disagreed on the best option. This nonprofit had a designer volunteer who had developed six logo options. Each was lovely in its own way. As a matter of procedure, the following question was posed to the team: "Do you have the brief you gave the designer or even the goals you had for the logo?" The answer: No. It was just an attempt to "freshen" the logo. There was no real goal. No criteria. And this was round four of development! Of course they were having trouble. They were running a race with no clear finish line. Indeed, the lack of a brief might reveal more systematic issues related to a lack of strategy. In today's increasingly competitive communication environment, the winner isn't a result of pure chance. Rather, those with strategy win and those without strategy fade into obscurity.

Now, a clear and obvious solution to this first shortcoming is the development of a creative brief. The danger here is that simply having a brief does not mean you have a good brief. It is not enough to quickly slap a brief together. Developing a good brief often takes time. Indeed, we have heard clients lament, "We're rushed. We don't have enough time. This project is so small anyway." As the old saying goes, "a stitch in time saves nine." Weak or incomplete briefs lead to longer development time—always. In fact, a poor brief can give a false sense of security that might do as much harm, or even more, then no brief at all.

To address the issues, let's start with our first brief. Although brief formats vary, the brief we use in this book—which we use routinely in our teaching and consulting—focuses on six core components: objective, target, insight, positioning, execution, and measurement. The brief that follows provides a concise description of each of these elements.

THE CREATIVE BRIEF

OBJECTIVE	The goal the advertising or communication is meant to accomplish
TARGET	The audience intended to see or experience the execution
INSIGHT	A meaningful human truth about the target
POSITION	The statement of the brand's category and benefit
EXECUTION	Personality, Mandatories, Timing, Budget, and Media
MEASUREMENT	How the objective will be assessed in practice

As we progress through the book, each of the next six chapters elaborates and explains one part of the brief in greater detail. For now, consider the following brief for a fictional company we use as an example throughout the book: Stark Cloud Solutions. Stark is a cloud data storage company that targets businesses that need to safely back up and store their data.

STARK CLOUD CREATIVE BRIEF

OBJECTIVE	Increase sales of the Stark Cloud
TARGET	Potential Cloud customers
INSIGHT	Customers need to protect their data; the Stark Cloud offers the most secure data protection
POSITION	Stark Cloud has the greatest functionality, the largest community of customers and partners, is the most secure, the most proven operational expertise, and has a two-year warranty
EXECUTION	Show the Stark logo prominently at the beginning and end of the execution for three seconds
MEASUREMENT	Management approval. Sales increase

Is this a good brief? It is simple, to the point, and brief. However, even if you are unfamiliar with brief writing, you probably can find several areas for improvement. Take a moment to do so. Feel free to write in the margins of the book or underline what you believe is weak and what you think is strong. When you are ready, read the next paragraph. We'll wait for you.

Have you finished critiquing the brief? What did you notice? Let us share a few pain points that stand out to us. First, the goal is not specific. Second, it is debatable as to whether the insight is truly insightful at all; it seems to simply state a point of opinion on the category. Third, the positioning seems vague—what does it mean to have the greatest functionality? And there are five benefits. Should the ad show all? Is one benefit more important and therefore should be focal in the ad? What you have just read is a dangerous brief because, on the surface, it seems okay. The problem is, briefs that take this form—which we have encountered in our interactions with brands—lead to unclear advertising and rounds of development with no clear strategic core from which to judge.

9

So this is a bad brief. Let's scrap it and look at another iteration for Stark Cloud Solutions. What about the following brief?

STARK CLOUD CREATIVE BRIEF

OBJECTIVE	Increase sales revenue of the Stark Cloud by 5% in this fiscal year
TARGET	Small and medium sized businesses who are potential cloud customers
INSIGHT	Customers need to protect their data, but are nervous about upgrading; the Stark Cloud offers the most secure data protection
POSITION	Stark Cloud is the most secure cloud service
EXECUTION	Leverage Stark graphic assets. Primarily U.S. digital media
MEASUREMENT	Ad adheres to brief. Sales in Stark Cloud increase 5%

This brief seems to have improved, right? That's not a trick question. Yes, it's definitely better, not worse, than the original one. And this level of fidelity in a creative brief is fairly common in our experience. Certainly, many people might be satisfied developing a communication based on this brief. It is with this level of fidelity that our book really starts. Even the aforementioned brief can be significantly improved. We believe this book needs to exist for this very reason. Along the way we return to and draw upon this brief as an example and take it from good to great.

Finally, one more observation merits our attention. Even with a solid brief, a common error is the failure to seek or obtain *senior management approval* before starting creative work. On one hand, this failure is understandable—why add another layer of approval? On the other hand, here is what the former type of thinking misses. Anyone who will be evaluating the advertising or communication should see and approve the brief. Senior management will often approve the spending. However, as we have learned through many interactions, senior leaders are not always well versed in creative evaluation. Without their approval of the creative brief, you risk them not understanding or dismissing the creative execution after considerable resources have been put behind it. Help them and yourself by getting alignment at the start. This is not perfect protection against changing objectives or terrible feedback, but it helps.

Myths, Misconceptions, and Other Questions

In the final portion of each chapter, we consider common myths, misconceptions, and other questions related to the idea of a creative brief. These are direct or paraphrased comments and questions we've encountered from students, clients, and/or executives. We share these with you because you likely have—or will—encounter similar ones. Now you will have a better answer when asked.

"These strategic exercises are for old school advertising. In the digital age we move fast and test our way to success."

Yes, digital technology often allows us to engage in quick testing and multiple executions. But what executions are you testing? How did you decide to come up with them? How much money did you spend creating each execution? How much time did you spend developing and approving them? Are they even the right ads to be testing?

We find the strategic guidance a good brief provides has become even more valuable because of the content needs created by proliferating digital channels. As Marc Pritchard, the chief brand officer for P&G, observed, "advertising has a bad reputation as a content crap trap. In this digital age we're producing thousands of new ads, posts, tweets, every week, every month, every year. We eventually concluded all we were doing was adding to the noise." He's right. Without a strategic foundation we risk spending money simply to throw noise at our consumers or customers. Let's not add to the noise. And one of the single best ways to avoid this is to have the discipline to put together a creative brief. In fact, if it is not worth writing a creative brief you might want to step back and ask why you are bothering with the content at all.

"I need to let creatives be creative, not be constricted by a brief."

On multiple occasions we have been told that any input by the client is viewed as unnecessarily restricting the creative freedom of the agency. That is, people believe creatives prefer *not* to have a brief; the creative brief is viewed as a source of tension as opposed to a bridge. Such a perspective simply does not ring true based on our interactions with most agencies, especially the best ones. Consider the following anecdote. We once asked a copywriter if he would rather have a blank sheet of paper from which to start the creative development process. His answer: "Absolutely not." He explained that his task is to create ideas that help accomplish the client's objectives. While being directed how to do the creative work was not desired (e.g., "Make me an ad where a spotted dog tells an orange cat how good the food is!"), he viewed it as equally terrible to have no constraints. "There's nowhere to start," he said. "I want the client to fence in the yard. Make it big enough that I can create, but not so big that I'm not sure where to start." Great briefs help agencies do great work. And powerful, on-strategy work helps you achieve your business goals.

"Once the brief is written it is a contract and it should not change for any reason."

We have often heard that the creative brief is a contract and, as such, it should never be changed once written. In contrast, we view creative briefs as road maps, not indelible etchings. A creative partner might be able to help you see a more effective or easier road to traverse to your objective. As such, be open to feedback and discussion that can help make your brief better and more suited to accomplishing your objectives. Great creative briefs can arise out of an iterative process with an agency. If you need to "fix" the brief, change it and agree to it; that becomes the new standard. Be open to changes, not open to loose interpretation. If you are building a house and the builder suddenly suggests she has a better idea for configuring your kitchen, would you want to hear it? Probably. It's worth a discussion, but that doesn't mean a discussion has to lead to a change in the plan. The builder suggests you don't need a kitchen? Terrible—you don't need to change the brief. As we reinforce throughout the book, being open is not an excuse for bad brief writing. We will give you the tools to have a meaningful conversation and to incorporate good feedback.

"Do I really need a brief for a small project?"

You can and probably should scale the amount of research or resources devoted to brief development in alignment with the expense/importance of the output. However, small-scale projects are not an excuse to forgo strategy. More than a few times we have seen small content pieces get brands in hot water because the lack of understanding of their consumers leads them to offend or alienate their target! If it is a small piece of content, it may not need its own brief, but it should at least consult a larger campaign brief to make sure it serves a strategic purpose and you are not introducing unintended inconsistencies.

"More is better?"

"If I had more time, I would have written a shorter letter." this roughly translated statement from French mathematician Claise Pascal sums it up. Strong creative briefs are almost always a single page. The name even has "brief" in it. Writing a great creative brief is about prioritizing and distilling the most important information for the creative team. It also has the practical impact of helping the creative team focus. A key benefit of strategy is that it encourages and, in fact, requires prioritization. Thus, in developing creative briefs, including the one we use in this book via our Stark example, we aim for parsimony. Having a ten-page "brief"—which we have seen in practice—is often a sign that the "distillation" of much market research has yet to be properly done. Thus, rather than "more is better," a principle in creative brief writing is "less is more." Of course, the "less" still has to have the critical ingredients, and that is what we go through in the remaining chapters of this book.

When teaching, we end each session with time for students to quickly jot down their key learnings from the session. Thinking about what stood out most to you or what applications there could be to your current business helps cement the learning.

Objectives

. . . .

"Would you tell me, please, which way
I ought to go from here?"
"That depends a good deal on where you
want to get to," said the Cat.
"I don't much care where—" said Alice.
"Then it doesn't matter which way you go," said the Cat.
Lewis Carroll's *Alice's Adventures in Wonderland*

We can paraphrase the exchange between the eponymous Alice and the grinning Cheshire Cat as "if you don't know where you're going, any road will take you there." And this is a fundamental truth related to the creative brief: a clear objective is required. We have to know what the purpose of a communication is to both properly plan it and to ultimately gauge the success of the creative work. However, as we discuss in this chapter, for a number of reasons, setting a proper objective is easier said than done.

From another vantage point, imagine that we decide to host a dinner party. What is a successful party? Great food and great wine? Sure. An exciting theme or location? Possibly. An interesting and memorable experience? Probably. But wait, we are getting ahead of ourselves. Let's step back and think about the different reasons why we might host a dinner party. Perhaps the objective is to nurture relationships among old friends. Perhaps we are raising funds for a charitable cause. Perhaps we hope to sooth contentious work relationships. Or we might host a dinner party to broach the potential for a buyout with a competitor's CEO. We might host a dinner party for a variety of reasons. And as the purpose for throwing the party changes, so does the specific objective of the party.

Clients often think of advertising objectives like the party. "Let's just have great food and great wine" translates to "let's make a great ad." However, such reasoning is too broad and abstract; we need to have a clear eye to the end result to plan for success. Why do we need a more concrete objective? A clear objective affects how a caterer might plan the party. It provides guidance on who sits where, what food to serve, and how long the party will last. A proper objective also allows us to gauge success. For example, if the objective was to nurture friendships, success might be reflected by one or more guests extending an invitation to host a party in a month. If the objective was to ameliorate animosity, success might be measured by future interactions in the workplace.

In this chapter, we discuss how to set proper objectives in a creative brief and in an advertising or communication campaign. Core to this idea is that, while sales might often be the final objective for many firms, as strategists we need to be clear about the specific role the proposed execution plays in that process. Although advertising and communications can be directed at a promotion to increase sales; they often address issues that precede purchase, such as awareness or brand perception. The tighter the objective, the more focused the output.

Setting an Objective: The Basics

Where do objectives start? In most cases, the impetus for an advertising or communications project cascades down from an annual planning process. That is, at a higher level, an organization has set quarterly or yearly objectives. As part of this planning process, it is not uncommon to have an initiative to drive sales of a product or service in the upcoming period. As marketers or communication experts, we are tasked with discussing how communications can play a role in driving sales or other business objectives. Put differently, we have to ask what the objective of our communications is within the larger business objective.

To illustrate, consider for a moment that we are marketers in the beer industry. Our brand team might decide it is important to invest in the hard seltzer market. To do so, we may have an initiative of launching a new hard seltzer to the market and achieving a particular number of sales. As part of our marketing efforts, we might develop communications to increase consumer awareness of the product both at retail locations and at bars. Alternatively, instead of investing in the hard seltzer market, we might decide it is important to grow one of our well-known light beers by pushing its greater taste attribute. Here, the communication goal is not awareness; rather, the communication goal is forming or changing consumers' opinion or attitude toward our product.

At this point, it is useful to call attention to an important distinction regarding business and communication objectives. Driving sales of a product or service is a **business objective.** The end goal in most for-profit firms is to improve the frequency and/or amount of sales or some derivation thereof. However, many paths exist to achieve sales growth. We could increase sales by growing the overall market. We could increase sales by stealing share from a specific competitor. We could grow sales by increasing loyalty or usage frequency among existing customers. Depending on which path we take, our communications will have a much different job to do. An effort to raise awareness, change attitudes, or drive a particular action (e.g., word of mouth, visiting a website) is a **communication objective.** To be most effective, we would say something different to encourage current users to increase buying frequency than we would say to nonusers to prompt entry into the category. While an advertising campaign or a communication initiative can facilitate sales, it plays a more specific role and it's the strategist's job to identify that specific role.

To elaborate, think about objectives or goals this way. We have our business objective (sales, profits, share, etc.). This objective can, in part, be accomplished through the behavior change of our target audience—new entrants to the category, switching/stealing occasions from a competitor, increasing usage or maintaining loyalty of existing customers. Driving this behavior change often requires awareness or attitudinal barriers that a firm must overcome. For example—the target is not aware of our brand; the target perceives that our product is not a good solution for a certain occasion; the target perceives that a competitor is superior on a key product dimension. Our job as strategists is to isolate the most important barrier to overcome; this barrier is integral to our communications objective. When we write a brief, we are providing the specific goal the initiative for which we are writing our brief is meant to accomplish. Said differently, we aren't writing a business objective. We are writing a communication objective that helps the execution contribute to the business objective.

What makes for a good communication objective? Good communication objectives can be differentiated from bad objectives based on at least two properties. First, a good communication objective is **specific.** It should be focused on precisely what the message or execution is trying to achieve. Again, while sales might be a business objective, executions often attempt to facilitate that objective through some more specific means. As previously noticed, this is central to a communication objective—we focus on the most important barrier to overcome. A specific communication objective might center on one of a number of factors: awareness, product knowledge, attitude change, direct action, etc.

Second, a good objective is **falsifiable.** That is, it is empirically possible to collect data that can differentiate a successful and unsuccessful performance. We have often seen objectives written so that it is possible to find an angle or tell a story to validate the objective after the fact. For example, imagine we wrote our objective for launching our hard seltzer as "make people aware of our hard seltzer offering." What does awareness mean? Does it mean that a local news outlet covers our brand? Does it mean we get people to follow our social media feed? How many? Is it successful if forty-seven people (or more) become aware of our hard seltzer? An easy way to make an objective falsifiable is to have a specific objective (e.g., awareness, attitudes, an action) linked to a desired quantity (e.g., 5 percent lift in awareness; 20 percent change in trial). Moreover, precision can be added by binding this quantitative objective to a specific time period (e.g., 5 percent lift in awareness and 20 percent change in trial within six months). With these basic ideas in mind, let's discuss the value of setting objectives and how to be effective in doing so.

Value to Clients and Agencies

Understanding the distinction between business and communication objectives is important because it helps guide our agency or creative partner to create the most impactful work to achieve the specific communications objective. By achieving the specific communication objective, we in turn achieve the business objective. To understand the value of concrete objectives, let us start with an exercise we often use during our workshops with brands. For illustrative purposes, let's imagine we are working on a campaign for Tesla's automotive division and let us consider different objectives we could put in our creative brief.

Objective: *Make an ad for Tesla.* Yes, we've seen objectives that are as simple and concise as this one. However, let's be honest: this is really bad. We really should be ashamed of ourselves if this is what we have penned onto the paper of our creative brief. First, we have set a horribly low bar for our creative partner—we are basically saying anything will suffice! Imagine if we told the caterer for a black-tie gala that the objective was "to have food present." Are we really going to be happy if our guests are served mini hot dog links and stale potato chips? No. Objectives at this level are often a sign that inadequate thought has been given to the purpose of the communication.

WHAT'S MY OBJECTIVE?
MY OBJECTIVE IS FOR YOU TO MAKE ME
AN AD!

Objective: *Increase sales for Tesla.* We have moved on from just producing a piece of advertising. We have seen a lot of brands start with sales as the motivator for an ad campaign. However, when it comes to a creative brief, this is still bad. This objective says nothing about how much. Are we really happy if a multimillion-dollar campaign has a net effect of one more Tesla purchase? Definitely not. However, the lack of precision and a quantity is not even the most severe problem with this objective. This objective tells us nothing about how the communications objective is meant to help. Are we trying to increase awareness? Are we trying to change people's minds? Are we trying to tell people when or where to buy? Again, this is a classic error of stating business objectives in lieu of communication objectives; such behavior does little to help our creative partner or ourselves.

Objective: *Change perceptions about Tesla's suitability for driving long distances from 25 percent to 45 percent positive.* This is a much stronger objective. It is much clearer in terms of the role of our advertising campaign in increasing sales—by changing perceptions or opinions toward Tesla with regard to its suitability for driving long distances. We are using communications to facilitate the sales goals in a specific way; this objective gives the creative team a much more precise path to success. As a result, it also provides a means to measure success, a point we return to later in this book.

Let's return to the party analogy. "We want a great party where everyone has a good time" sounds lovely. But a "great party" will be massively different if it's meant for a new product kickoff for investors or a two-year-old's birthday. For a new product kickoff party for investors, a good party might be accomplished if investors want to put money behind it—this might lead us to feature the product prominently as part of the event. For a two-year-old's birthday, a good party might be accomplished if the entertainment helps fill the party with laughter—this might lead us to seek out a clown or a magician. Let us be clear: we almost never have the luxury of just making a great ad. We need an outcome to help guide the purpose of the campaign. So start with the end in mind. What will success look like after this campaign has the intended impact? What specifically does the communication at hand need to accomplish? Unlike Alice, we need to answer the Cheshire Cat by saying exactly where we want to go.

Forcing ourselves to look hard at the objectives offers brands several other benefits. First, we have found that a serious examination of objectives can reveal situations where advertising is not warranted at all. All too frequently we have seen brands fall into the trap of doing advertising just to "do" advertising. This leads to reusing the objective from last year and having the agency create more ads without any real value. For example, if we succeeded in changing consumers' perceptions of Tesla's suitability for long distances so that consumers now understand that point, that's unlikely the correct objective for the following year!

Setting a proper objective means we also have a bar to measure our success or failure after the campaign has run its course. If we do not have a specific communication objective, then we do not know if we succeeded. This hurts us on many dimensions. It deprives us of the ability to critically learn from both our successes and failures. Indeed, having a clear marker of success versus failure is one reason managers writing briefs are reluctant to make a strong objective. That is, they do not want to exhibit failure or have a means to realize they have failed. However, as we elaborate momentarily, this is flawed logic as learning from failures can be one of the best ways to achieve future success.

Finally, with increasing cost pressures a number of agencies are moving to a base retainer plus bonus structure. Agencies are rightly hesitant to tie bonuses directly to a client's sales because of the myriad of factors besides advertising that can impact sales. By developing clear communications goals, we also have clear criteria for a bonus-oriented compensation structure.

Why Brands Fail and How to Succeed

So where do brands get it wrong and how can they succeed? First, as we have already noted, many brands set either too vague of an objective or no objective at all. One reason people fail to do so is that they do not want to be proven wrong. Being clear in our objective can mean we sometimes have to accept that we failed. People often do not want to recognize they failed, nor do they want management to realize they failed. However, it is only through the recognition of failure that we can learn from our mistakes and build a more successful communication strategy moving forward. In practice, trying to make a failed campaign look successful can lead to a vicious cycle where, instead of one failed campaign, you are left defending an unsuccessful concept for years. Eventually, no matter how hard one tries to hide it, that long-term failure will become undeniable. Recognizing short-term failure can prevent long-term failure. No campaign is perfect. Great marketers recognize and accept limitations and failure rather than mask failure as success.

Another concern is that without a clear objective, the creative team ultimately inserts their own objective. They might insert an objective such as *let's make something award-winning* or *let's make something highly entertaining*. Those might be great additional accomplishments, but the reason we are spending all this money is to accomplish a communication objective that will help support the business. Thus, doing due diligence helps us avoid a creative partner setting their own objective and instead helps them focus on what we need to achieve. Agencies need to know what we want to have happen as a result of the work. When our creative partner is clear on the objective, we have another set of minds thinking about how specifically to reach our goals.

Another reason for failure is that brands sometimes set the wrong objective. In particular, they set goals that advertising can't accomplish. Frequently the problem is that we are using advertising to address a problem best suited to another tactic. We once worked on a brand with terrible loyalty numbers. Consumers tried it once and never returned. The problem was that the product didn't deliver on the benefits required of the category. The brand manager requested a new ad campaign to "fix sales." The product was doomed for failure because of its poor quality, and advertising is not a salve for a broken product. The point here is simple. Objectives cannot reflect goals that advertising cannot solve. Imagine a laundry detergent that didn't clean clothes. Would you buy that product again? No! There's an old saying in advertising—"The fastest way to kill a bad product is with good ads." Thus, strong brands set objectives that advertising can solve; this is a path to success.

Revisiting the Brief

. . . .

Let's revisit the creative brief for Stark Cloud Solutions from our first chapter—the second version that we declared an initial improvement. Our original objective in this brief was:

| OBJECTIVE | Increase sales revenue of the Stark Cloud by 5% in this fiscal year |

This appears both specific and falsifiable. On the surface this objective reflects some of the major requirements of a solid objective. So far so good! However, while we aren't totally off, it's not as strong as it could be. We haven't given any direction to what the communication itself should accomplish to facilitate this business objective. Let's fix this.

First, let's add specificity to our objectives. Let's make clear what the business objective is versus the communication objective. The business goal is to increase sales by 5 percent. However, sales might increase for a variety of reasons; we need to know how our execution will facilitate this objective. Again, a communication objective identifies exactly what our advertising is meant to accomplish. In this example, let us assume that from some focus groups we know that we have to tackle a very common perception barrier—that cloud data are not secure. Only 15 percent of the potential customers we spoke to perceived our services as secure. As such, we can state a very concrete communications goal: we want to achieve a lift among the perceived security of our services from 15 percent to 35 percent. A good marketer can tie anticipated business results to a well-focused communication objective.

Here is the revised objective:

OBJECTIVE	Increase perceptions that Stark Could "cloud has the most secure data protection" from 15% to 35%"

Can you picture in your mind the different ads the agency might create when given the original objective of increasing sales by 5 percent? Maybe. The possibilities are immense, as is the variance in our chances for success. When we change the objective to focus on perceptions around data security, it should be easier to have a clearer idea of what a successful ad might look like. An ad will have to communicate something that leads people to walk away with a shift in how secure they see our services. We also have a clearer idea of how we might measure the success of this ad—that is, do we observe a change in how many customers agree we are secure? Unless you are like Alice, you do care where this effort is going!

This simple exercise has allowed us to take the average fidelity we see in an objective and make it into something far more meaningful. This is how we should be writing objectives in our brief.

Myths, Misconceptions, and Other Questions

"How do you know what the barriers are to overcome or which to prioritize?"

This is one of the toughest jobs of the marketer. Where should we focus? At the heart of this question are two pieces: identifying the issues and then prioritizing. Typically, marketers use some form of qualitative research (interviews, focus groups, social listening, customer service feedback) to identify the most prevalent barriers to usage. In our Stark Cloud Solutions example, the 15 percent may have come from our sales force who told us that only 15 percent of customers they spoke to actually believed we were a secure option.

The next step is prioritizing these barriers. What impediment, if overcome, would lead to the greatest positive impact for the business? For prioritizing, we can leverage quantitative research to understand the scale or prominence of these barriers within our target customer group. Perhaps a survey of potential customers revealed that "security" was the dominant driver in choosing a cloud data provider. Finally, we must evaluate the likelihood a given tactic will be able to overcome these barriers (i.e., can we succeed?).

We touch further on these issues in our discussion of targeting, insight, and positioning (Chapters 3-5).

"How do you get to the levels of specificity that you reached in your examples?"

This is a good question that we get a lot. Let's take our example: *Increase perceptions "Stark Cloud Solutions has the most secure data protections" from 15 percent to 35 percent among our target.* This is usually measured in some kind of larger, quantitative survey of the target audience. It might be measured as part of a broader survey that measures awareness levels first and then attempts to understand the perceptions about your brand and the competition.

To be more concrete, the sales force might ask target customers the following question during a call before (pre-) and after (post-) a marketing campaign:

Stark Cloud Solutions has the most secure data protections.

1 – Mostly disagree

2 – Disagree

3 – Neither agree nor disagree

4 – Agree

5 – Strongly agree

By tracking perceptions before and after exposure, we can have a sense of how the campaign affected perceptions. Alternatively, we can track the perceptions among an exposed group and an unexposed group during an ad campaign. We dive into such measurement issues later in this book (see Chapter 7).

"Shouldn't the business goal be part of the objectives?"

This is a very common question. Our perspective is that the business goal should drive the communication objective. It is the job of the strategist to make this link. This is difficult and requires a prioritization of potential options as stated earlier. This focus will then drive many of the remaining elements of the brief. As such, one doesn't have to have the business goal in the creative brief itself. Keep in mind that the creative brief is a specific communication document; it is fine to have other documents besides the brief—for example, an overarching marketing plan likely communicates the sales objective.

Of course, some companies choose to include the business goal as well as the communication goal in the final brief deliverable. To illustrate, going back to our example of Tesla, we could easily write the objective as: *Increase sales of Tesla by 8 percent by changing perceptions about Tesla's suitability for long distances from 25 percent to 45 percent.* While we do not see it as necessary, for brands that desire it, we see it as acceptable to include the business objective in the brief. However, if you do so, make sure to include the specific communications objectives of this initiative. The mistake we see all too often is people fixate on the business objective and, once that is on the brief, they do not go the extra step of mapping out the communication objective.

Finally, we have both found that translating the business goal into the simplest possible terms will be most helpful to your agency and quite often your own team. A brand of mayonnaise wanted 5 percent growth in a flat market. We looked at bringing in new users versus increasing the consumption of existing users. The brand had an enormous existing user base, and it was difficult to talk new people into mayonnaise or to steal users from the competition (i.e., very high barriers). So we did some simple math to understand exactly what behavior change and associated knowledge change were needed to achieve the business goals.

For example, let's assume the mayonnaise producer needs something close to 15 percent of their user base to buy one more jar of mayonnaise a year to hit their sales goal. We broke it down further—that meant approximately four hundred thousand existing users had to make one more sandwich a month with the mayonnaise. So our business goal was translated into the more tangible idea of encouraging four hundred thousand existing users to eat one more sandwich a month, and the communication goal was to increase knowledge of other mayonnaise-based sandwich recipes from an average of two to four. Do you know how much easier it is for the team to get their head around that level of specificity versus "grow sales 5 percent?" Can you start to imagine the kinds of tactics that might help the brand as you read this?

Target

. . . .

People and firms are different. Some spend more; some spend less. Some are more loyal; some are less loyal. Some are easier to reach; some are harder to reach. People and firms also have different needs. Some people try to portray an image; some people seek functionality. Some firms are focused on growth; some firms are focused on retention. People and firms also have different preexisting perceptions about your offerings, your competitors' offerings, and the category. You hear a lot of academics talk about the heterogeneity among consumers and firms—that's just a fancy word for saying people are different.

Ed Sheeran ✔
@edsheeran

I can't tell you the key to success, but the key to failure is trying to please everyone

Here is the reality. As a marketer, whether we are marketing consumer-packaged goods, a high-tech firm, a nonprofit, or a business-to-business manufacturer, we are faced with an important decision. With the abundance of differences between people, we have to figure out who to target for our campaign. Indeed, as the quote by Sheeran cited earlier elegantly elucidates, trying to please everyone *is not* an effective tactic. In fact, it is neither financially nor creatively viable. In this chapter we explain both why we need to specify a target and how we can accomplish this successfully in our brief.

Selecting a Target: The Basics

At one level, selecting a target—or targeting—is intuitive: given the vast differences among people, we have to identify the specific group of people most likely to allow us to achieve our business objective. And the identification of the target often influences our specification of the communication objective. As intuitive as this is, it turns out choosing an appropriate target is often a complex process. The complexity arises from the fact that, as highlighted at this chapter's outset, not all potential consumers or businesses are the same. Because different targets have distinct needs, they require tailored communications. As such, as strategists we have to find an appropriate target so we can understand their needs and design our message to move them to help meet our business objective.

To facilitate targeting, we often start with segmentation. Most marketers have heard of segmentation and they understand the core idea. However, a vast difference exists in understanding a concept and truly appreciating and knowing how to implement a concept. Certainly, it is not uncommon for brands to understand the idea of segmentation but to have very little understanding of the segments that exist in the marketplace. Without understanding the segments that exist, it's hard to proceed with proper targeting! So let's start with the concept of segmentation. Segmentation is an exercise used to divide a specified population into mutually exclusive and, to the best of our ability, collectively exhaustive groups. Proper segmentation for a marketer is like creating a map. We sketch out the topology of the different territories to capture differences in the size, shape, and unique characteristics of each region.

Ideally, we cluster groups of people or firms in a segmentation based on shared needs. We do **"needs-based"** segmentation because a critical aspect of marketing is solving the needs of a specific population to achieve business goals. Segmentation by needs provides the path by which to accomplish this objective. In practice, this becomes difficult because needs are not easily observable in a population. For example, most people cannot look at a consumer and say, "Mark really cares about how well his detergent protects his colors," or "Diane cares about whether the detergent has a natural and fresh smell." As a result, we often turn to proxies for consumers' needs. One approach is to use geographics (e.g., Midwest, urban, etc.) or demographics (e.g., age, company size, income, gender, etc.). Or, to get even closer to the needs we can rely on behavioral (heavy users, nonusers) or psychographic (attitudes, beliefs) segmentations. All of these help us direct our advertising toward consumers with a shared need or **insight**, a matter we discuss in the next chapter. However, at its core, proper segmentation helps us understand the territories on the map and what differentiates and defines them in terms of their needs.

Once we have drawn our map, whether targeting consumers or businesses, now we have to select who to target; this decision represents the move from segmentation to targeting. Here is the reality: targeting is about **prioritization**. Imagine we had an entire year to travel wherever we wanted in the world and we had a budget of a million dollars. Sounds great, right? Even with an entire year and a million dollars we cannot see the entire world. It is too vast to successfully traverse given our generous but limited time and money. In marketing, we rarely, arguably never, have the resources to reach every region on the map we have created in our segmentation analysis. Thus, we need to prioritize and figure out which regions merit our resources.

Here we are confronted with a natural and important question as clients: what makes a specific target preferable or desirable? For us, a desirable target is one that will best help us achieve our communication objectives in the service of our business goals. If our goal, for example, is to obtain a million new users by changing perceptions, then we need a target that is sizeable and for which such growth is plausible. This is one of the reasons why having a concrete objective, as discussed in the previous chapter, is so important. The concrete objective allows us to evaluate the potential value of different targets. Proper segmentation allows us to evaluate each target and understand where we can offer the best value (i.e., fulfill a target's needs better than the competition). We need to create value for our target(s) and in turn our target(s) must create value for the company and collaborators (e.g., help us meet objectives).

Can we have more than one target? If we have the resources—time and money—then it is possible to have more than one target. In our discussion of myths, misconceptions, and other questions at the end of this chapter, we elaborate on this issue and on approaches to multiple targets. However, as we discuss in the coming chapters on insight and positioning, we need an insight for each target to shape our messaging. In addition, different targets might require different media channels to reach them in an effective fashion. Indeed, as we move from one target to another, we often need separate creative briefs for each target. For now, we focus on identifying a first and primary target and how to represent the target properly in the brief.

To summarize, as a client we often have to answer two questions when selecting a target. First, we have to understand the lay of the land; we need to have a reasonable assessment of the target opportunities available to us—this is known as segmentation. Second, we need to make the decision of how to prioritize the regions we have identified—this is known as targeting.

This prioritization often involves finding the target that provides the path of least resistance when it comes to reaching our objective. Ultimately, the selection of the target involves weighing trade-offs. We have to advertise to some customers at the expense of not talking to others. Targeting focuses our limited resources on the group of people who are more likely to create value for us—so we have to choose a target!

WE DO HAVE A DEFINED TARGET, WE'RE APPEALING TO
RETIRED YACHTERS, GIFTED TODDLERS, URBAN RODEO
WRANGLERS, AND BUSY MOMS.

Value to Clients and Agencies

On the surface, the value of targeting to the client is easy to explain. Imagine that we are a toothpaste brand and that we want to increase our sales of toothpaste by 20 percent with a $2 million ad campaign. One target we could pursue consists of students who have just entered college and are choosing for themselves, perhaps for the first time, which toothpaste to use. We could spend $2 million on media channels to reach this target. Alternatively, we could pursue current users of a competitor—Crest toothpaste. These individuals love Crest toothpaste and are very reluctant to give it up. We could spend $2 million on media to reach this target. However, we cannot effectively reach both targets with $2 million. Who do you think is more likely to be persuaded by this message? We know you know the answer is the first group—there are fewer obstacles for us to overcome. However, while this observation is simple in form, it illustrates the importance and undeniable value of targeting for the client.

Although targeting is easy to understand in its basic form, targeting as a strategic concept starts to have real teeth when it comes to the brief for the creative and media agencies. First, for the creative agency, the target helps them craft a message designed specifically to compel and persuade this audience. Second, the media agency will use this target to select and purchase media channels. Both of these are important functions to understand, so let's unpack each.

First, on the creative side, the role of the agency is to create a message so influential that our target audience 1) attends to the ad to completion amidst everything else vying for attention in their environment, 2) understands and internalizes the message, and 3) changes perceptions and/or behaviors specified in the communication objective. Not an easy task. This is why most clients engage with agencies that have specialists—the creatives— geared toward this difficult task.

Second, targeting also has implications for the media agency. What is a media agency? Most firms with substantial advertising budgets hire a media agency that handles media planning and buying. Media agencies are experts in getting the message to the target consumer in a specified channel. This media agency might be housed within the same holding company as the advertising agency—such as Leo Burnett and Starcom under Publicis—or it could be an independent agency. Regardless, the key role of the media agency is to put our advertising, content, and/or communications in front of the right people at the right times and in the right places. And, when it comes to media buying, what was once an art has become much more of a science. The media team will often use a program that inputs campaign goals, target parameters, and budget to make recommendations about the media buy. Fundamentally, sound media buying is about reaching the right people, at the right times, in the right channels. We discuss these factors, as well as media decisions, in greater detail in Chapter 6.

Thus, beyond helping us use our dollars effectively, the target portion of the creative brief is highly informative to both the message that will be created and the media that will be purchased. In fact, the target will ultimately be linked to an insight and position, which we discuss in subsequent chapters.

Why Brands Fail and How to Succeed

Let's talk about why brands fail when it comes to targeting. We will share with you three common targeting errors that we like to think of as the "everyone target," the "popular kid target," and the "egocentric target."

To start, perhaps the most common error we see is the **"everyone target."** This error takes the form of a brand specifying no target or a target so large and amorphous that it does not help prioritize the message or the media dollars. This error generally stems from a failure to appreciate the basics of segmentation and targeting. For example, this error arises when firms have not done a proper segmentation analysis and, as a result, all the targets look alike. We were once having a conversation with a business-to-business brand, and we asked them who their target was. They replied, "everyone in the industry." That's the entire map of potential targets, but that is not a target! This error also arises because, while a firm has done a segmentation analysis, they are unwilling or unable to prioritize targets. We worked with a global phone company that when pressed to narrow their target for the launch of a new phone "acquiesced" to five separate and wholly distinct groups with very little in common. This is not a great outcome for the brand or the agency. At its core, targeting is fundamentally a means to concentrate resources against the specific group most likely to respond to the communication objective to fulfill the business objective. The best ad feels like it is made just for you. The broader firms go in describing their target, the broader and more watered down the message and media plan become.

A second targeting error is the **"popular kid target."** After analyzing the segments, firms often uncover "the best" target with respect to the largest group using the category or the group most willing to spend in the category. For example, a former student of ours was leading the marketing efforts of the popular parking app SpotHero—an app that helps consumers find places to park in crowded areas. Examining the potential customers, the student found that occasional leisure parkers were the largest segment and had the lowest historical cost per acquisition. On the surface, going after the obvious target seems sensible. Why wouldn't you want to spend on the largest target or the group that spends the most in the category? The problem can be summarized in one word: **competition**. Usually, the obvious target is also the one being highly advertised to by your competitors or better served by your competitors. Indeed, for SpotHero, the parking locator app market was crowded with new entrants who all saw the same thing. While they all competed on price for this target, our student focused his firm on serving the second most attractive and underserved target, the business parker. Fast forward five years and they now have a leading market position.

Does this prior discussion mean you always have to forgo the popular target? No, if you are the leader in the category, or the first to acquire a target, you might be the one to own that desired target. Or, if you truly have a unique insight about them, you might be able to win them over relative to the competition. However, in many cases, going after the obvious target overlooks underserved targets where growth could be achieved with greater ease. For example, the Old Spice brand had tried to target young men who wanted to attract women. The proposition was clear: Old Spice helps you smell attractive to women. Young men who want to be attractive to women is a large target. The problem was this target and position were owned by a larger and more powerful brand, Axe. As such, Old Spice pivoted to target young men who wanted to feel confident. No brand was talking to the group with this need. This pivot in the psychographic need of the target—from attracting women to feeling confident—caused Old Spice to move from no growth to triple digit growth.

Finally, it's crucial to keep the target in mind when evaluating the advertisement. The third marketing error is focusing on the **"egocentric target."** We use this term to capture the idea that people often think about who will like the ad with respect to themselves. However, in many cases, you are not the target! Indeed, we have had former students marketing to kids or males marketing feminine hygiene products. You need to ask who the target is and then evaluate the ad through her eyes. Think about what else she is watching. What else competes for her attention? Is your message relevant to her? Will this break through the clutter of advertising? By way of illustration, once we were reviewing an ad for a confections product targeted to teen boys. The attendees in the room included no such young men. Before showing the ads, the agency showed clips of the most popular TV shows, online videos, and other content with which the target was engaging. That was crucial in helping us better evaluate the advertising.

In short, choose a target for your communications that is large enough to accomplish your goals, but as tight as possible in order to provide specificity in your message and media. Be right for the right target. Or as British

songsmith Ed Sheeran articulately and aptly notes: "I found a love....
for me."

Revisiting the Brief

Let's revisit our creative brief for Stark Cloud Solutions. Our original
target was:

TARGET	Small and medium sized businesses who are potential cloud customers

That has some specificity. It's not all potential cloud customers. We've
narrowed down the territory on our map to small and medium-sized businesses. This probably accounts for some knowledge we have that customers
of large enterprises prefer Microsoft and Amazon solutions; Stark Cloud
is at a disadvantage in this space. But, according to the US Small Business
Administration (SBA), we have narrowed it down to 30.2 million businesses
or 99.9 percent of the businesses in the United States alone. Would we tell
our sales team, "Okay, 30,200,000 potential customers. Start making calls"?
We wouldn't want to waste their time, and we don't want to be inefficient
with our advertising. Let's see if we can get closer to the most likely target
segment.

TARGET	SMBs from $50MM to $150MM in sales whose existing servers are reaching 5 years in age

Here we have tightened the target segment most likely to need our
product. We have also added another level of specificity—the age of the
existing hardware storage servers. We know that the average life span of a

server is five years, so these firms should be most likely to consider a switch to the cloud. We have identified a trigger correlated with their entry into the market. The size of the company in sales and the age of their servers is information that can often be procured through research or by buying the data.

Myths, Misconceptions, and Other Questions

"Why do I need one target? I can use digital technology to do micro-targeting with personalized messaging (aka doesn't digital kill the need for a target?)."

Remember targeting is prioritization. Advertising to multiple small segments can be productive as long as the benefits outweigh the costs in media, production, and people's time. Having a single, strategic target is still valuable because it helps us make decisions apart from advertising. What price should we charge? Where should we sell? What features should we develop next? A single, clear, strategic target can guide the brand to more optimal decisions.

Gender, age range, income levels, education, and purchase behavior are all tactical markers that help the media agency determine the size as well as how to find this target. Specificity in targeting becomes somewhat of a trade-off for media. Typically, the more general the targeting characteristic, the less expensive the impression and the broader the population. As we narrow down, we use additional data sources that we own or purchase to find things like past purchase behavior.

Moreover, because of all the data available, brands can go down the rabbit hole of specificity until they are reaching minute audiences at a very high price. In practice, we've done exercises where the cost to micro-target far exceeds the incremental sales it facilitates. Once we ran a micro-targeting test for a retailer where we broke the existing customers, who were already a fairly narrow target segment, down into micro-segments in order to understand whether that "deep segmentation" would drive better responses to promotional emails. After testing twenty-some variations, two segments within their existing customers proved worthwhile—male and female.

A good media agency will find the right balance between cost and specificity. That is, specific enough to be effective, but not so overboard clients are overpaying for specificity that goes past usefulness. In the end, we want to guard against splintering our resources and focus.

"What if we have multiple targets?"

As noted earlier in this chapter, it is possible to have multiple targets. Indeed, more established firms often have multiple campaigns with each developed for a different target. However, even in such cases, it is about a subset of territories on the map; it is not every region. In both business-to-consumer (B2C) and business-to-business (B2B) marketing, firms might have a new growth target, but also want to maintain sales from existing users. As targeting is prioritization, a firm can rank the segments by importance. A helpful framework we use to visually represent this prioritization is a bull's-eye.

Targeting Bull's-eye

We start by asking which segment is the primary target for an advertisement. They might be the primary target because of their size, our ability to persuade them, or the fact that the competition has not advertised to them. That target goes in the middle in "Own." Which segments can be tactically pursued at a lower cost and with less resource drain? We recognize these secondary segments in the second ring, labeled "Attract." Finally, other segments will buy from us without warranting special attention, shown in the third ring, named "Accept." While a firm may need to balance multiple targets, for any given advertisement, the greatest chance of success comes from a singular target. And, given a limited budget, a point exists where additional targets are not feasible. Another way to think of the bull's-eye is that, when it comes to research allocation, it is a pyramid—the "Own" target gets the most resources, the "Attract" target a more moderate amount, and the "Accept" target the fewest.

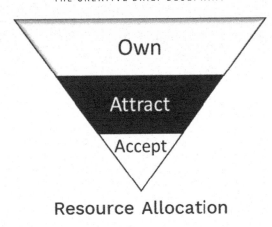

Resource Allocation

"Isn't it risky to go after a smaller target versus a larger one?"

This might be the most asked question in our targeting discussions with executives. "Won't I have better luck fishing in the ocean than in a pond?" Most find the answer we give counterintuitive. For decades, mass targeting was the strategy. After World War II, as mass media rose and national retail chains grew, firms would find success making a product that was good for most people, telling everyone about it, and carving out precious aisle space in the mass retailers. Barriers to entry were high and everyone was satisfied with the options presented.

However, in the 1990s, globalization and advances in production efficiency started to reduce barriers to entry in manufacturing. Digital platforms then dramatically lowered barriers to entry in online retail and allowed for much more specificity in targeting. The happy middle, where firms could be "okay" for many, was attacked from all sides by firms choosing to be great for few.

Many markets are now seeing historically famous brands erode as customer segments find new offerings that are better designed, communicated, and delivered to meet their specific needs. If you stop and think for

45

just a moment, examples will come to you. Don't be okay for everyone, be great for some.

Insights

· · · · · · · · · · · · · · · ·

Let's start this chapter with an assignment. Go find a piece of advertising for a product or service for which you are a relevant target, but it does not move you toward purchase. This task should not be hard. If you need some help, turn on the television and wait for any local advertisement for a home improvement service, a furniture store, or a retail store. Open up your web browser and do a few online searches. Watch some YouTube videos. Did you find something? If so, great: keep it in mind as we work through this chapter. If not, or to complement the advertisement you have in mind, we will supply you with an example.

Consider a video execution on YouTube for a furniture store called Grand Furniture. The ad quickly cycles through a variety of its furniture offerings; it touts low prices, high quality, extensive variety, and style. With so much to offer, what could possibly be wrong with this advertisement? You sense the sarcasm, right? Good. Here's the problem. In the previous chapter, we put a great deal of emphasis on prioritization. If we are going to go through all the effort to prioritize a target—which we should—we now need to message to this target effectively.

Messaging to a target effectively begins with understanding **insight**. We need to understand our target's pain points and needs. A core problem with the ad for Grand Furniture—and possibly the one you found—is that it explains what the brand can offer, but it fails to identify and focus on what is going on in the mind of the consumer. It is simply speaking at consumers; it is not a response to consumers' needs. We think of insight

48

as the glue that binds the target—discussed in the previous chapter—with the position—discussed in the next chapter. To understand the nature of this powerful adhesive, let us dig deeper into what is meant by an insight.

Understanding Insight: The Basics

What is an insight? We have both asked and been asked this question multiple times. To us, the idea of an insight can be captured in a simple but powerful definition: an insight is a **meaningful human truth**. Let us break down each component of this definition.

The first part of an insight is that it has to be **meaningful**. "Meaningful" has two critical elements. First, an insight must reflect value to the consumer that can be tapped so as to motivate belief or behavior change. For example, consumers might appreciate that their new sports car comes with embossed floor mats. However, advertising the inclusion of the floor mats may not have any true meaning that would change their attitudes or behavior.

Second, an insight should not reflect the regurgitation or reapplication of the same knowledge that all competitors have. In many categories, an insight reflects the discovery of a truth about the consumer that is of value and that competitors have not utilized. In some cases, an insight can be the rediscovery of a truth that has been forgotten or not utilized in advertising for a period of time.

If we dig into the etymology of the word, the earliest reference appears to be in Scandinavia around 1200 CE: *innsihht*, meaning sight with the "eyes" of the mind. A later sixteenth-century definition likened an insight to "penetrating understanding into character or hidden nature."[1] These definitions reveal what we need in advertising and put a spotlight on the importance of the insight being meaningful. Now, by meaningful, we want to be careful to not equate insight with counterintuitive, mysterious, or previously undiscovered; not all insights are groundbreaking discoveries. Sometimes it is simply a matter of being the first brand to understand and capture a rather sensible need in a target. For example, Axe body deodorant revolutionized the deodorant category by creating a strong association between young men wanting to attract women and its ability to facilitate that goal. The idea that their target wanted to attract women would not be considered an astonishing revelation. However, Axe shifted the conversation in the category from performance and endurance to something that tapped a meaningful and unleveraged insight.

The second part of an insight is that it is about the target—it is **human** focused. A mistake we see all too often is that brands want to make the insight about the service or product they provide. We understand the temptation. We want to be loved and we want to share all the wonderful reasons for our consumers or customers to love us. The problem is that telling consumers what we can do is part of our message or positioning;

---

1   Source: https://www.etymonline.com/word/insight

this is not an insight! We have to tell them what we can offer based on what they need. To illustrate this problem, let us recount an experience a friend shared with us. She was shopping for bicycles. The sales associate went to great lengths to explain all the benefits of the bike—lightweight aluminum frame, airless bike tires, and additional bells and whistles. The sales associate, triumphant he had messaged the product effectively, finally asked if she had any questions. She responded, "Do you have red bicycles?" The sales associate was so focused on selling the product that he was focused on the wrong information.

The final part of an insight is that it has to be a **truth**—that is, it has to reflect an accurate observation about the consumer. A brand might find or extract an insight from a focus group that seems both meaningful and human but ultimately is wrong. For example, we were once working on a packaged meat brand. Consumers in a focus group mentioned they had a greater perception of quality when they could see the meat they were buying, not covered in packaging. So far so good. Other competitors did not have transparent packaging, which made this potential insight meaningful, and it certainly was about the consumer. As such, this led the brand to change the product packaging to be transparent so that consumers could see the meat. However, the problem was it was not true. Once the product was put in the market, most consumers actually did not prefer to see the product. They liked the nontransparent packaging that showed the food in an assembled sandwich.

As the example in the prior paragraph illustrates, consumers do not always know what they want. As such, in many cases, we need to dig deep to make sure what appears to be meaningful and human is also true. We have also seen brands fall into a particularly malicious trap of the following form. Some brands focus so much on developing a message around their offerings that they fail to ever consider or extract an insight about the consumer or customer. However, rather than admit they have no insight, they make something up to fill in the insight portion of the brief. They create something that is about the consumer, but it ultimately is either not meaningful, not true, or both. This approach is a bad idea.

For example, an entrepreneur we know once increased the colors available for an electronic product accessory on his website. He did so because he believed that consumers would prefer more variety in color and his competitors did not have a high degree of variety. The problem is while this was meaningful in terms of the competition not having thought of it, it was a false insight because it was not true when it came to what consumers cared about. We have both seen campaigns whose failure can be linked to the lack of a true insight. It is not worth taking time to fill out the insight purely to "check the box." If you are going to leverage insight—which you should—then you need to invest in actually finding one. And if you are not going to leverage insight, you are better off not pretending to have one—just leave the box blank.

I CAN SENSE THAT YOU HAVE
A DEEP TO DESIRE....TO HAVE....YOUR FORTUNE TOLD.

With the idea of a **meaningful human truth** in mind, let us take another look at the Grand Furniture execution. Did it provide an insight? First and foremost, there is nothing particularly meaningful in the execution. It is just a laundry list of what the product offers; it does very little to identify a meaningful need in a target. Indeed, it isn't different from most furniture commercials. Moreover, the advertisement does little to demonstrate an understanding of the consumer. It is not about what the consumer needs or wants; it is about what the brand has to offer. If you do not have an observation that is meaningful or about the consumer, you cannot even judge the veracity because there is no insight! Do you still have the ad you thought of from the assignment at the start of this chapter? If so, test what you see against the definition of an insight. Is there an insight?

Now you might be thinking that insight is hard. Besides, what possible insight could one have about furniture? Finding a great insight is hard, we agree. However, difficulty is not an excuse for lack of insight. You can have great insights even if you sell furniture. Consider a classic example of insight featured in an IKEA advertisement called "Lamp." This ad, directed by Spike Jonze, features sentimental music playing in the background. The audience sees a woman remove a "Pixar-esque" weathered lamp from her desk and walk it out to the cold, gray curb for garbage removal. We are witnessing the end of a twenty-five-year relationship. We're moved. We're sad. As we watch this poor lamp sitting on the curb in the rain, our thoughts are abruptly disrupted by the appearance of a Swedish man who addresses us as follows: "Many of you feel bad for the lamp. That is because you are crazy! It has no feelings and the new one is much better." What just happened? That funny Swedish man standing in the rain just called out a meaningful human truth keeping some consumers from replacing some furniture. Put simply, some consumers, perhaps without conscious thought, kept some furniture pieces past their useful life because of a sentimental attachment the furniture cannot return.

Value to Clients and Agencies

. . . .

Today, marketers can much more easily track the behavior of a target audience, especially online. For example, we can observe when someone visits our site, clicks our ad, or abandons a shopping cart. And we can survey people to ask about their perceptions and brands and the category. Which brands do they know? Which brands do they like? What products will they buy next? But the real magic for a brand comes when it understands why consumers do what they do and why they feel the way they do about the brand, the competition, and the category.

Insights are incredibly valuable to both clients and agencies. For clients, as we noted, insight is the glue that binds the target and the brand position. Put differently, insight provides the impetus for us to build the positioning for our brand. For agencies, insight allows them to understand how consumers think and feel and this can facilitate their creative development. Consider the Snickers advertising campaign built around the insight that "you are not you when you are hungry." The campaign featured individuals who momentarily did not look like themselves—for example, young adults were replaced by older actors—until their hunger was satisfied by Snickers. This insight captured a common consumer experience of not acting like yourself when distracted by hunger.

This insight served the client well because it allowed them to offer a solution consistent with their equity—Snickers satisfies your hunger. Snickers is a candy bar made with peanuts, caramel, nougat, and chocolate and boasts one of the highest calorie counts per serving in the category. Snickers could have gone with something simpler such as great taste. But ask yourself, does that feel unique to Snickers? Are those obvious benefits something that another candy bar could not offer? This "you are not you when you are hungry" insight opens a space to connect with customers that actually fits with the product's calorie count and historical equity.

This insight also served the agency well because it allowed them to offer a provocative way to demonstrate the insight and the benefit. One ad—run during the Super Bowl—featured a football game in which one of the actors was beloved older actress Betty White cast in the midst of young twentysomethings. After a botched play, a team member turns to her and says, "Stop playing like Betty White." Betty White is given a Snickers bar and suddenly is transformed back into a young male player—that is, his normal self. In doing so, the brand demonstrated it understood consumers' needs (i.e., you are not you when you are hungry), and it demonstrated how the brand solved this problem (i.e., Snickers satisfies your hunger and returns you to being you).

Insights are also extremely valuable because, as we have noted, consumers cannot always articulate why they behave a particular way. Consumers don't always know how they want their product packaged, for instance. As a consequence, brands that invest the effort to obtain insights have a competitive advantage. As an example of the difficulty consumers have articulating them, consider the IKEA furniture ad we mentioned earlier. If we asked you why you don't buy more IKEA furniture, would you really tell us, "Well, I have a potentially illogical sentimental attachment to this couch I purchased after college." Not likely. In fact, you might try to generate alternative reasons; you might say that you have the furniture you need, the prices, the convenience. Therefore, while we might try to message around our prices or convenience this message will have little traction because it is not tethered to a meaningful insight.

Consumers can also fail to fully understand, and thus are unable to articulate, why they made a highly involved and "logical" purchase such as a new car. "Why did you buy the Tesla?" Concerns about the environment, fuel savings, strong safety record, interest in the technology, tax incentives? These aren't necessarily untrue, but that's not why some people bought the car. It's a cool car that goes really fast, and we've wanted something like that since we were five. This observation merits elaboration. Consumers—whether it be focus groups, surveys, or online reviews—are not intentionally trying to mislead marketers. The complete set of reasons for their actions is sometimes actually unknown even to consumers; thus, when pressed, they attempt to generate a logical response. The logical response given is not always the real motivator. As such, brands and agencies need insights to design messages that are actually effective.

Let us share one more example of a brand that recognized the power of an insight. Specifically, we'd like to share with you a particularly valuable insight revealed by the Luvs disposable diapers team at P&G. Context is important here. P&G already owned the higher-priced, category-leading Pampers brand of diapers. According to P&G, more than 25 million moms in one hundred countries use Pampers every day. Luvs needed to find growth without the resources of its sister brand and without stealing consumers away from another P&G brand. What was the brand to do?

In the new mom category, there's no shortage of underlying emotions around their new baby. However, Luvs realized that consumers' behaviors shifted when the second child entered the family. The "second time moms" were much more likely to purchase the value-priced Luvs. When the brand team dug in, they found that the increased confidence with baby number two led to all sorts of different attitudes and behaviors—from less stress about germs to feeling smarter about the choices they made in baby care. Luvs brought this forth in a humorous series of ads showcasing new moms versus second-time moms that ended with the line "By their second kid, every mom is an expert, and more likely to choose Luvs than first-time moms." You can see the insight coming through. And as these parents were already prone to shift away from the higher-priced Pampers, Luvs was not at risk of cannibalizing its sister brand.

Why Brands Fail and How to Succeed

. . . .

Given the tremendous importance of insight, it might come as a shock that brands routinely fail on this dimension. One reason for the failure is that it is often difficult to find a valuable insight. Doing so requires time and money. And it sometimes requires patience; insights are rarely discovered overnight or in a single meeting. Moreover, as we have noted, one of the hardest hurdles in finding an insight is that humans aren't great at exposing them. As advertising giant David Ogilvy said, "Consumers don't think how they feel, say what they think or do what they say."

Now, if we are lucky, we sometimes have the assistance of specialists on both the client side and the agency side to navigate the difficult process of discovering an insight. On the client side, we might have an "insights" team or a "voice of the customer" team. These research pros can be essential allies. On the agency side, there is a role that also acts as the voice of the customer, traditionally called the account planner. An agency account planner can be of tremendous assistance in developing the creative brief, particularly in finding the right insight.

We often need expert help because we must navigate past the obvious and less meaningful responses of consumers to the underlying "why." It can take a deft touch to dig in this far. Our colleague Jim Stengel, former CMO of P&G, has a wonderful quote: "If you want to understand how a lion hunts don't go to the zoo. Go to the jungle." Yes, traditional surveys and methods can sometimes reveal the thread of the insight. However, there is something special about being with consumers in the wild, walking alongside them as they shop in the grocery store or talk about their weight loss tricks. Great brands succeed because they invest in studying human behavior.

An illustrative example is warranted. Once we were trying to learn more about one of our breakfast products—a delicious fully cooked and flash frozen breakfast sausage. Sales were lagging even as we touted the main benefit in ads and on packaging. "Just microwave for 60 seconds and have fresh breakfast taste fast with no mess." We knew we had effectively communicated the benefits of "microwave ready" and "taste" because they scored well in surveys. Consumers told us that these were important benefits, but the problem was these benefits were not the ones that truly drove consumers' behavior.

Then we conducted an ethnography—we ventured out into the wild. Two members of the brand team were sitting at the kitchen table of someone's home at 6:45 in the morning while family members straggled into the kitchen for breakfast. Mom grabbed the sausages from the freezer, popped them in the microwave for a minute, and then put them in a frying pan!

What was happening? The whole point was that she didn't have to do this; she just needed to use the microwave. It says so right on the box! Had we failed in some simple communication? No. She had a clear motivation, which she explained. Cooking in the pan, however briefly and technically unnecessary, turned the action from "warming" to "cooking." "Warming" in the microwave is just a functional task, but "cooking" in a pan is an expression of love for her family. We followed up to see if this was an isolated incident, and it turned out the "finishing in the pan" behavior was widespread. This insight not only changed the communications around that product, this insight also altered how we thought about new innovation. Helping moms save cleaning one pan is not much of a benefit; allowing moms to express love more often because we make it easier to do that at breakfast is a heck of a benefit. This also illustrates the balance between art and science that leads to great insights. Data are useful. Sometimes we see an irregularity that leads to an insight, and quantitative studies can help validate the breadth of an insight. But more frequently insights come in through noticing and investigating subtle cues from our customers. Arguably, there's no better way than spending time with our customers in the wild.

A final observation we have found useful is to be very careful in using "what" versus "why." "What" is an observation, a piece of data, a fact. It's buying value-priced diapers with a second kid. It's cooking precooked sausage in pan. An interesting "what" is the thread that you need to pull on to find the insightful "why." **"Why"** is buying value-priced diapers because you have more expertise and feel more in control as a parent; it is cooking precooked sausage to feel you are expressing your love to the family. Thus, when you observe something that surprises you—a what—start pulling on that thread until you get to the why.

Revisiting the Brief

. . . .

It's that time of the chapter when we revisit our creative brief for Stark Cloud Solutions. Our original insight was presented as:

INSIGHT	Customers need to protect their data, but are nervous about upgrading; the Stark Cloud offers the most secure data protection

The best part is that we have already shifted the focus from what we provide to what they need. We have a potential start to a revelation here about the "why" behind not upgrading to cloud. This will certainly help our creative partner too. However, we have really just scratched the surface with a fact—customers need to protect their data. This observation is still shallow, but there is a thread—people are nervous about the upgrade. But we're not sure why. Let's make it better. To move this insight forward, we would likely meet with customers and have conversations. Let's assume we have done so, and we are now able to represent the insight as follows:

> | INSIGHT | The target is frustrated by the costs and resource requirements of internal storage. However, they continue to use internal storage because they fear that cloud data storage is unsafe and will be compromised |

Here we have more depth in two respects. First, we now articulate **why** they are frustrated with their current situation. They find it expensive and draining on resources to maintain the hardware servers. More important, we now understand the largest barrier preventing them from upgrading to cloud services. They fear that cloud solutions will lack the security they need compared to their own internal options. This insight reveals the obstacles we need to overcome. Can you now see how the insight can become the glue between target and positioning? Do you see more clearly what we would say to this target if we had ten seconds of their time? If things are a little fuzzy still, don't worry. We will work on using this insight to inform our positioning in the next chapter.

Myths, Misconceptions, and Other Questions

"A valuable insight must be something that has never been thought of before."

This is a myth. Not only would this put a pretty high bar on efforts to find something useful, but it might lead to overlooking easy wins. Remember that an insight is a means to better connect your offering to your target customer. A well-worn trope such as "moms are busy" is an overused insight and likely will not best serve your brand. However, Axe's use of "attracting a mate" may be one of the oldest insights in human history; yet, because they were the first to leverage it in a novel way against their target, they were able to build a successful brand that outshined the competition for years. Similarly, we can all relate to the idea that we aren't ourselves when we are hungry. Snickers saw an opportunity to be the main candy bar to use this as fuel for their award-winning and highly successful advertising campaign.

"Insights are for consumers; they don't apply to B2B brands."

In general, people ask us if the creative brief, and the insight in particular, is applicable for B2B brands. To avoid ambiguity in our response: yes, yes, and absolutely yes. Even in business-to-business marketing you are interacting with people, and insights surround and govern their attitudes, perceptions, and behaviors.

Let us share a great example from a former student. Our student worked for a firm that developed electronic tags to avoid theft at retail stores. These are the tags attached to clothing and products that sound off when a consumer "accidently" forgets to pay and tries to exit the store—it happens. Our student's firm marketed security products to North American retailers. Through observing and interacting with his customers, he realized that they all had an amazingly similar pain point. Specifically, on Black Friday—the busiest and wildest shopping day of the year—they were in a lot of stress. He formulated the insight that they really needed a bit of reprieve and peace of mind. He decided to address this insight by sending both current and prospective customers a "Black Friday Survival Kit." The kit, delivered around Black Friday, had all the items the retailer needed to survive—coffee, an energy drink, junk food, a stress ball, and, perhaps most important, samples of the brand's product to prevent the headache of retail theft. Our student had a real insight about the customer and the response was phenomenal—almost every retailer who received a package responded with a personal phone call or email! His marketing effort both retained current customers and brought in new ones!

It also bears mention that the idea that retailers are stressed during Black Friday is not surprising. However, our student was the first to actually put this insight into use and message around it. Indeed, a number of the retailers would exclaim how his was the only firm that had ever reached out to help them navigate Black Friday!

"Insights are a creative writing exercise."

Sometimes people spend too much time "wordsmithing" an insight. Rather than focusing on whether they have a meaningful human truth, they want a slick expression or phrase. Remember, our creative brief is not consumer facing. The consumer never sees the creative brief. The creative brief is our road map to great communications. Spend the time getting to a valuable insight and then communicate it clearly, not poetically. In working with your agency, they may suggest changes in wording to make your brief simpler, clearer, and even more inspirational to the creative team. Hopefully they do! The key is to make sure that none of these adjustments change or undermine the core strategy.

"A meaningful human truth must reflect a behavior common to all humans."

This myth often goes hand in hand with the idea of boiling the ocean when it comes to targeting. Few insights are universal—the idea that young men want to attract females does not apply to all males! The insight that some consumers are too attached to their furniture does not apply to fashion-forward consumers who seek designer furniture (and, perhaps surprisingly, these aren't IKEA targets either). Instead, the specificity you brought to the target can help you here. The insight must be about your specific target. And by being specifically focused on your target and not generically broad, your insight can have much more power.

NOTES

Positioning

. . . .

"The difference between the almost right word
and the right word is the difference between
the lightning bug and the lightning."

Mark Twain

This chapter explores the heart of our message: positioning. A simple but powerful way to think about positioning in communications is as follows. Positioning is the main message that you want the target to take away. As Mark Twain observed, an immense difference exists between positioning done right and positioning done *almost* right. In classic marketing strategy, a brand will attempt to find a positioning or "position" that is valuable to the target, owned by the brand and not the competition, authentic and believable, and worth building upon for the long term. Great brands have consistently stood for something that people find important, and with that consistency comes easy associations in consumers' minds when a need arises that a brand can satisfy.

One of our favorite quotes on the topic of positioning comes from Steve Jobs. It was 1997 and Jobs had returned to Apple. In an internal meeting revealing the first commercial of the new "Think Different" campaign, he shared the following observation: "This is a very complicated world, it's a very noisy world, and we're not going to get a chance to get people to remember much about us, no company is, and so we have to be really clear on what we want them to know about us."

Over the years, whether it is products, physical locations, or service offerings, the Apple brand has come to occupy a distinct space in most people's minds. Apple created a message around their brand associated with creativity that seamlessly integrates form with function. Moreover, these rich associations with Apple transfer to new products. These powerful, differentiating associations also allow Apple to charge a premium with service margins of more than 60 percent and iPhone margins at more than 35 percent. In essence, this is what we attempt to capture in this chapter: developing a brand position that resonates with the audience and builds your brand for the years to come.

Selecting Positioning: The Basics

We have worked through a lot of exercises with brands on writing a positioning statement. A positioning statement is meant to provide a concise summary of how a brand is to be represented in a communication. Here is an example of a positioning statement we might write if we were opening up a new chain of coffee shops—called Rutigue—focused on a customized experience.

To coffee patrons with discriminating tastes (**Target**), Rutigue is the upscale coffee shop (**Frame of Reference**) that offers consumers' taste buds a customized experience (**Point of Difference**) because we have thirty unique beans we grind right before your eyes (**Reason to Believe**).

Let's unpack this positioning statement. Our positioning statement has four critical pieces of information that we have placed in **bold.** It tells us who it is for (Target), what the competitive set is or who it is better than (Frame of Reference), the main reason for choice or why we are desirable within that set (Point of Difference), and why our proposition can be believed (Reason to Believe). See the image that follows for a graphical representation of these ideas.

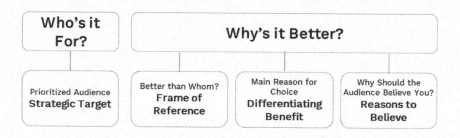

At its core, our positioning statement is engineered to answer a singular question—why should our target choose our offering over that of the competition? However, in practice, writing this positioning statement is no easy feat. It's difficult because we have to distill our messaging strategy into a single sentence.. Every word requires vigilance to avoid missteps or vagaries. A concise but meaningful positioning statement shines a clear light on the path ahead for success. To start, let's break the positioning statement down into its core elements to understand the role each plays.

Target. The target is essential because the relevant benefits will differ by target segment because of unique insights. As promised, the message we communicate—or our positioning—follows from the insight we have about the target. Of note, while the target is listed on the brief, we often have discussions around positioning outside of the brief. This is why we like to include the target in our positioning statement. In an actual creative brief for Rutigue, because we have identified the target in its proper section, we may simplify the positioning statement to:

Rutigue is the upscale coffee shop (**Frame of Reference**) that offers consumers' taste buds a customized experience (**Point of Difference**) because we have thirty unique beans we grind right before your eyes (**Reason to Believe**).

You probably noticed we kept the terms **Frame of Reference**, **Point of Difference**, and **Reason to Believe** in bold. You might be wondering, "But if you are writing it as it appears in the brief, wouldn't you remove those descriptors?" Actually, no. We routinely keep them because that forces our clients to identify and check that each one is properly represented. In some cases, we might remove them from a final version of our creative brief to keep it concise for the creatives, but as strategists, we would certainly have them in our first drafts! Now, let's take a moment to elaborate on each part of the positioning statement.

Frame of Reference. The frame of reference is an essential but often woefully overlooked part of a strong positioning statement. The frame of reference is the competitive set. The easiest way to think of it is as follows: if the target does not use your brand, what brand, product, or service are they using instead? One key issue people fail to understand is that the frame of reference is malleable. That is, a marketer can represent the same product or service in different categories (within reason) to best represent the brand to a target.

To illustrate what we mean by this malleability, consider Hyundai's launch of the premium sedan Genesis in the United States. Hyundai could have launched it as another Hyundai product and represented it in the category of "family sedans." Instead, introductory ads showcased the vehicle's luxury attributes and featured it in traditional luxury settings (e.g., upscale hotels). Hyundai wanted consumers to mentally "place" this offering in the category of "luxury sedans." Hyundai used the advertising to create a frame of reference of "luxury sedans" as opposed to "family sedans." Why does this one-word difference matter? Because, as Twain astutely observed, that one "right word" means a lot.

Membership in the luxury category did three things for Hyundai. First, it created a new path to growth for Hyundai. With no other vehicles in that class, Hyundai aimed to steal market share from a different category and avoided cannibalization of its own offerings. Second, consumers already have some associations with categories such as luxury sedans. By associating itself with membership in an established category, a brand can immediately assume some of those associations. If we tell you the Genesis is a luxury sedan, you might immediately generate assumptions about the price range, a quiet, comfortable luxury interior, and advanced driving capabilities. And you might assume this without Genesis explicitly stating any of that. In short, the proper frame of reference gives consumers an amazing amount of information in just a word or two. Finally, understanding the frame of reference in which you are competing helps you find the differentiating benefit that creates an advantage for your brand in customers' eyes relative to other choices. For example, Genesis is a luxury car priced 30 percent below similar models. The price tag won't be an advantage versus mainstream models, but against the frame of reference of luxury cars, this can be powerful for the targeted buyers.

Point of Difference. The point of difference represents the key differentiating benefit of a product or service. This point of difference or benefit is often derived from some insight about the consumer or customer that the brand can deliver on. What makes for a good benefit? We find that a good benefit often has four critical ingredients, to which we alluded at the start of this chapter. Specifically, a strong benefit is:

1) valued by the target (i.e., tethered to an insight)

2) ownable by the brand, not yet strongly associated with any competitors

3) authentic and accurate

4) has staying power to build the brand for years to come.

Now, while many benefits exist, we have found that most if not all benefits can be placed into one of two broad categories: **functional** versus **emotional**. Functional points of difference or benefits explain what a product does for you. For example, North Face makes cold weather outerwear. BMW provides power and exceptional handling on the road. The Apple watch keeps track of your health and fitness, allows you to answer calls, and allows you to pay with Apple Wallet.

Although important, especially for young brands or new products, functional benefits are only one means for brands to distinguish themselves. As a brand matures, it often seeks to create an emotional connection with consumers by linking the function to an emotional experience. For example, by protecting wearers of the brand from cold weather, North Face allows outdoor enthusiasts to excel at their passion. By offering superior performance, BMW allows drivers to feel empowered. Emotional benefits can offer another layer for brands to differentiate themselves from competitors. While a lot of products can keep you warm, North Face's advertising remains differentiated because of tapping into an emotional benefit.

One way to visualize the difference between functional and emotional points of difference or benefits is that they are part of a "benefit ladder." The benefit ladder is a tool brands use to help them understand if a more functional message or a more emotional message is best suited to a given situation. Think of the ladder as all the benefits offered by your product, from the chromium steel alloy bolts all the way to the sense of confidence that your machines instill in the businesses that use them. We start at the bottom with **Features**. These are true, observable facts about your offering. Maybe your childhood education nonprofit has six locations, retains five PhD counselors on staff, and is bilingual. Then we "ladder up." We ask, "So what?" What do those assets allow you to produce for clients in terms of a functional benefit? Perhaps the functional benefit is that children in your program learn to read 30 percent faster than those outside the program. Sounds good—let's take it up again to the emotional benefit. "So what?" Children who learn to read well early have greater confidence in school, allowing them to achieve at higher levels. And we can continue going up. We might even move further up on the emotional scale to **higher-order** benefits that represent a degree of self- or human actualization. Success in high school leads to greater success in life, and we can offer a better chance at a happy, successful life from six locations to the promise of a better future.

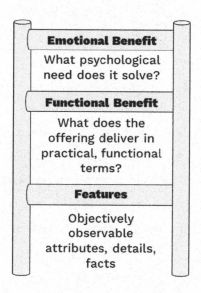

The Benefit Ladder

This ladder is incredibly useful to marketers because of the many places content will be needed. While a specific ad may focus on one higher rung of the ladder, the web site may be organized to showcase lower rung attributes, or the social feed may highlight each in turn. Choosing a specific rung for a given communication requires us to go back to the criteria for prioritization. Communicating any given point will not be helpful unless the audience finds it compelling. Per our criteria we shared earlier, this means the benefit 1) is valuable to the target, 2) is owned by the brand, not the competition, 3) is authentic and accurate, and 4) has staying power to build the brand for years to come. What we do in workshops with firms is to build out the ladder in depth and then score the brands' desired and actual performance on each rung. When ambiguity remains there is always testing, but we find this helps firms narrow in on the most important areas.

Reason to Believe. The reason(s) to believe reflects the data or evidence to support your point of difference or benefit claim. You're the most effective detergent? The most dependable cloud network? The safest car? Why should the target believe you? For example, when Cheer advertised the power of color guard, it did so through a side-by-side comparison of the color of a shirt washed with Cheer color guard and a laundry detergent without. The benefit was protecting the color, and the reason to believe was the scientific test. Lower rungs of a ladder frequently identify these reasons to believe and/or how they might be presented in advertising. And in practice, it's not uncommon for a brand to run multiple commercials each highlighting a different reason to believe in support of the main benefit. For example, the Leo Burnett agency advertised freshness as a functional benefit of Green Giant vegetables. Different commercials called out different reasons to believe this benefit such as the fact that the vegetables were handpicked, vacuum sealed, or frozen while fresh.

Value to Clients and Agencies

· ·

As we discussed in Chapter 2, we utilize advertising to achieve communication objectives. Communication objectives could focus on the awareness that the brand exists and is associated with a particular category (i.e., the frame of reference). They could help people understand the benefit (point of difference) of the product. They might be used to offer more support for the benefit (i.e., the reason to believe). Thus, it is possible that a given advertisement might have communication objectives associated with a specific part of the positioning statement. However, across a campaign we typically have to be vigilant that the full positioning statement is communicated to the target.

Of importance, once we have a strong positioning statement, everything in our advertising campaign is in the service of delivering that message. The entertainment value. The celebrity spokesperson. The dazzling event. The breakthrough execution on a new social media platform. The point has to be the message. Make it clear. This should be the heart of the creative execution, and it's why we are making an ad.

Practically speaking, clients will need to evaluate multiple executions. With a clear positioning statement, choosing an advertisement becomes easier, both as you evaluate rough ideas in the beginning and much later if you go into consumer testing. In testing, one question usually measured is the main "takeaway" from viewing the execution. If you are not clear about what that is, how could a consumer watching it be? Thus, positioning becomes one important tool to evaluate creative output. To that end, we return to the role of positioning in creative evaluation in Chapter 8.

In interactions with agencies and specifically creative teams working on ad development, clear positioning frequently arose as an issue. While all the aspects of a brief are important, the central crux of any communications is the intended message. Creative teams are trying to craft a story in order to tell a message in a compelling way. When the benefit in the brief is unclear, there is no real starting point. When the benefit is not one benefit but five, there is no clear path. Ideas stall when the positioning is unclear.

In 2013, the Blackberry mobile phone company ran an expensive Super Bowl spot that featured a man walking down the street with his phone. First, he bursts into flames, then he grows elephant legs, explodes into colored dust, and changes a crashing semitruck into a thousand little rubber ducks. The ad ends with this voice-over: "In 30 seconds it's quicker to show you what it can't do, the new Blackberry Z10." That's an agency with a big budget and no point of difference. The ad was largely viewed as a failure, and this can be linked back in part to bad positioning.

Why Brands Fail and How to Succeed

As we noted, writing strong positioning statements is hard. Indeed, we've done full workshops devoted solely to the positioning statement. Most people won't have a great positioning statement out of the gate. However, with repetition and refinement it is possible to create something powerful, persuasive, and persistent. Put simply, the path to success is difficult, but reachable.

To succeed, a great positioning statement should be both strategically sound and practically simple. Strategically, you are associating your brand with something that your target values enough to influence their choice. And you can own this benefit more strongly than the competition in their mind because of either an actual advantage or the perception of one. If building the perception of an advantage sounds like some kind of nefarious manipulation, it's not. Communications should never lie or deceive the target. We are not claiming a benefit we don't offer—we strongly discourage such behavior for legal and ethical reasons. Rather, we are representing our ability to deliver that benefit in a way that resonates with the consumer. We are owning some truth in consumers' minds. Dove owns "moisturizing." Do other brands moisturize? Yes. Does Dove moisturize better than every other brand and product? Probably not. Has Dove ensured that their communication has consistently reinforced this message so that most consumers strongly associate the moisturizing benefit with Dove? Yes. This won't work if the benefit you are trying to own is inauthentic to your brand. Practically, it needs to be clear and simple. First the agency has to understand it and then they have to explain the benefit through an ad to everyone else. Let's look at the most common errors.

Overpacking the position. One of the most common mistakes is clients cannot decide on which point of difference to advertise. This conversation often begins with a statement like "There are so many good things about us we just can't decide." We better. There are two possible outcomes. One is that the agency chooses one of the five benefits we listed. Is that the right one? There's a 20 percent chance. The other option is that the agency tries to communicate all five benefits in one piece of communication. Now the ad is convoluted and the target will remember none. We need to do the work ahead of time. And if we do not know what benefit to use, there is a place to look—we go back to the insight. What is the core insight about the target? That insight should drive the choice of benefit.

AND FASTEST...AND CHEAPEST...
AND SAFEST...AND....

Let the agency develop the positioning. We wholeheartedly recommend involving the agency in the brief development, but do not abdicate your role as the captain of the brand. There are classic anecdotes of the agency just happening upon the exact right benefit without a clear strategy. They got lucky or had a hunch. It can happen. The problem is those stories are the 1 percent (or maybe even smaller); you don't hear about the other 99 percent where the agency spins in circles presenting one idea after another that "doesn't seem quite right" and then launches something ineffective because the main benefit was never nailed down. This book, creative briefs, and advertising are not about getting lucky. They are about materially increasing your chances for success. Do your research on the most compelling positioning before the briefing.

Revisiting the Brief

· ·

Let's revisit the positioning piece from our creative brief for Stark Cloud Solutions. Our original positioning was:

| POSITION | Stark Cloud is the most secure cloud service |

The best part is the brevity. No overloading here. We have a frame of reference implied—"cloud service." Clearly communicating a frame of reference gives the intended audience information about our brand. Membership in a category implies that we have the same basic features and benefits as others brands or offerings in the category. And we have what should be the most important element—security. Even better, we are claiming superiority on an important benefit, which is powerful. But based on previous insight work and utilizing the positioning framework, we can make this more meaningful and impactful while still keeping it fairly parsimonious.

| POSITION | Stark Cloud is the data storage service (FOR) that is even safer than your internal storage (POD) because of its industry-leading encryption methods (RTB) |

Our target knows of cloud storage, but, as we discussed in the previous chapter, they are held back because they fear it is not as secure as their hardware. Being the "most secure" cloud server might not be helpful. Stark could still be less secure than their existing solution. Knowing that insight, we position not against other cloud servers, but against all data storage. We need to beat their internal hardware solution, which as it so happens, we do! The frame of reference becomes important. Our sales will come from users leaving hardware storage solutions and moving to cloud servers. That leads to a point of difference that meets their greatest need against the competition. And finally, importantly, we substantiate our claim with a strong reason to believe—our industry-leading encryption. Look at the transformation from an okay positioning statement to a positioning statement with real kick to it. This evolution is what we should aspire to.

Myths, Misconceptions, and Other Questions

. . . .

"Emotional benefits are better than functional benefits."

No rule says higher-ladder emotional benefits are always better than functional benefits. We have found that the determining factor is what's most meaningful, different, and authentic to your audience. Remember, insight is the glue between the target and the positioning. Yes, emotional advertising can create a strong bond, and telling a story that connects is powerful. But consider an ad from Google that ran during the 2020 Super Bowl called "Loretta." An older man dictates memories of his deceased wife to his Google Assistant. Very powerful, but very functional benefits are communicated as well.

In another example, we were working on a start-up for a premium-priced fruit smoothie that used "ugly" produce that would otherwise be discarded. The owner wanted to focus the advertising on the purpose of the company—removing waste from the food supply chain. We will not argue against anyone pursuing the greater good with their firm. The problem is this approach was not effective when it came to persuading the target; they weren't concerned about the higher-order purpose of an unknown brand. They wanted to know if the smoothies tasted great and what varieties were available. As this example illustrates, the greater good is not necessarily the most meaningful, ownable, and authentic benefit to convey to a target.

We have found that brands are frequently forced to go "up the ladder" for two reasons. First, the target consumers' familiarity with the features and functional benefits grows over time to high levels. You can reinforce, but without innovation at these levels, you aren't communicating anything new. Second, the lower rungs are the ones most easily copied by the competition. As all competition offers the same features and attributes, they become part of the category frame of reference and are less helpful to communicate. So brands move up until they find a place that is meaningful, ownable, believable, and worth staying with.

Apple is known for creating memorable emotional ads. But look at an Apple ad for a new version of a device. The ad will be highly functional. The lower-ladder features and attributes are not well known, and thus Apple will ensure that it communicates these points for new products first. Thus, the choice to ladder is a strategic decision that must consider the value of doing so based on a firm's current position in the marketplace.

"How do you balance Masterbrand and product-specific advertising?"

How should we balance the overarching brand, say, Caterpillar versus communications of the specific product lines underneath that brand, Caterpillar Excavators? The balance of Masterbrand versus product line support varies by firm and category, and it is driven by the specific needs of that business. Research from Binet and Fields suggests a sixty-forty split between what they call long-term brand building and short-term product-focused support. Of course, this is a heuristic and the split may depend on factors such as competitive context, one's prior advertising efforts, and customer insight.

Most successful firms spend years trying to find the right balance. Dove launched the "Campaign for Real Beauty" that was a higher-ladder emotional benefit, but also needed to communicate the new moisturizing capabilities of its latest shampoo. They have shifted the balance back and forth over the past decade, measuring the impact. It's not easy because the Masterbrand effects are more long-term versus the easy-to-see short spikes of product-focused activation. It's a synergy.

"How long do you keep a positioning or an ad campaign in the market?"

The short answer is as long as it accomplishes your objectives. Marketers are notorious for abandoning campaigns because they tire of them before consumers do. Of course they are tired of it! They see it every day. Consumers don't. While there are no hard rules for length, we can offer some initial guidance.

A brand's overarching positioning should be built for the long term; we often hope for an extended period of time—eight or more years. Of course, if the target changes, the competition changes, or an incredible opportunity opens up, we think about changing. Underneath this **Masterbrand positioning**, you can think about having three more "levels of positioning." First is the **advertising campaign**, a central creative idea that shares similar elements—Mac versus PC for Apple, Flo for Progressive, the Geico Gecko. These campaigns ideally run for three or more years. We want the consistency of elements to increase memorability. Change hesitantly.

Underneath a campaign, firms generally have an **annual focus**. In the annual plan or marketing plan for the year, specific objectives have been identified and communications are developed to achieve those goals. The lifetime of these actions is usually tied to accomplishment of goals, but generally they last about a year. And finally, we have the **individual ads** or creative executions. The useful life of any ad is fairly limited because after a certain number of audience viewings, the utility of that ad fades. Consumers have seen it, are aware of it, and have taken away whatever message was intended. We call this wear-out. Media agencies can give guidance on the approximate number of exposures when wear-out is most likely to begin, but a multitude of factors contribute to wear-out—including the creative itself, the audience, the message complexity, and the category competition—that prevent a nice simple rule of thumb. If you remember nothing else, change a campaign when you must, not when you tire of it.

"Do you really need a differentiating benefit, or can you focus on being the first brand to come to mind?"

In the past ten years, there has been some talk in the marketing world of abandoning the differentiating benefit and to instead focus on brand popularity. Basically, use advertising to build high top-of-mind awareness and a rich set of associations about the brand. We think that building high awareness and rich associations about your brand makes sense. Within these rich associations, we would argue, it nonetheless remains beneficial to give your customers a reason to choose your product or service over the competition. In many categories, similar brands with similar prices live side by side. The problem is, when consumers perceive no functional or emotional difference, price becomes the tiebreaker. When you are forced to compete solely on price, you are entering a downward spiral that will end in low margins at best. As our former colleague Sonia Marciano says, "When differences between firms disappear, so do profits."

Execution

· · · · · · · · · · · · · · · · · ·

Let's start with a short role-playing exercise. You are a famous executive and you have just been given the script for a surefire blockbuster—*Star Wars Episode 12: The Legacy of Vader*. The characters are fantastic, the locations surreal, the story line epic. You seem to have it made. The primary strategic decisions are essentially in place, but at least one more thing has to happen for it to succeed: the movie must be made. Even with the strategy in place, you still have a substantial number of tactical decisions to make.

First, you will have to set the tone of the movie. Do you want this Star Wars film to take a more humorous angle that features cute droids as in *The Return of the Jedi*? Or is it a return to something dark and serious such as *The Last Jedi*? Figuring out this tone will be critical because it will likely affect who you choose to direct the film, the casting decisions they make, the musical score, and how the film is shot.

Second, you will have to consider whether you will have any mandatories—that is, rules that the director must follow. Star Wars movies always start with a scrolling text prologue and then a consistent sweeping score. For a continuation of the saga, it might be sacrilegious to not include such items, which makes them mandatories for the director. The movies are also family friendly; there is no swearing or strong sexual content. These are all good things to note now as you seek out your director.

Third, you need to set a time line and budget. When will the movie be released? Next December? Three years? How big of a budget will you allocate? If you are planning for this to be a summer blockbuster—and you better, it is a Star Wars movie, after all—you might allocate $250 million to produce the film, a lot more than the $15 million you would spend for an artistic film or documentary.

Finally, you will need to make some media decisions in terms of where audiences will see the film. The film market has splintered into a multitude of ways to reach consumers. Perhaps *The Legacy of Vader* will go into theatres first followed by early home access on Disney+ before finally being released for digital and physical purchase.

Now, you might be thinking that being an executive producer sounds hard. To be honest, we cannot say for sure, but we suspect it is. More important, this role-playing exercise serves as an analogy for the type of decisions that we have to make as clients with regard to our advertising. And these decisions are encapsulated in what we call the "execution" section of our brief. Specifically, in this chapter, we dive into four pillars related to execution: **Personality**, **Mandatories**, **Timing and Budget**, and **Media**.

Execution: The Basics

Let's remove ourselves now from the role of executive producer—sorry if you find that disappointing, but we need to focus on the creative brief. We first take a look at the general notion of brand elements and how they relate to execution. Then we elaborate on the four pillars that constitute the execution section of our brief. Our goal is to make each pillar clear and actionable to help you understand how to write them effectively into a brief.

Brand Elements

A brand is a set of "elements" or associations linked to a name, mark, or other symbolic cues in consumers' memory. These associations can be neutral, positive, or negative. For example, a particular segment of consumers might associate Taco Bell with the color purple (neutral), with being inexpensive (positive), and being of lower quality (negative). Said differently, if we break this idea into pieces, we have 1) all the elements that signal to a consumer "this is the brand," and 2) the equity—good and bad—associated with the brand. In advertising, we try to leverage or optimize both. We need to leverage existing brand signals so that consumers easily identify the ad as coming from our firm—these aid with recognition and awareness. And we need to reinforce these cues by consistently employing them and then build and reinforce the equity elements associated with our brand—this helps with attitudes and action.

Within these cues are often elements that we would want to include in our ad or even an experience we're creating: the name, the logo, often the use of a consistent tagline. But great brands also leverage more subtle elements: music and sounds, colors, style of imagery or photography, and spokespeople. In fact, outside of advertising brands employ a range of cues such as touch, smell, and sound in their retail properties or physical experiences. Indeed, consider Disneyland, where each part of the park is kept immaculately clean, there is a waft of the appropriate cuisine, and there is music playing. Disney creates an amazing experience on its premise that is essential to its brand.

In the US, Orbit gum rose to number one in the category through leveraging an offbeat but effective campaign. Every ad featured a simple and ridiculous setup of a person becoming somehow dirty while their teeth remained clean. No matter the plot, every ad had sky-high brand recognition because every ad consistently included multiple brand cues. The same spokesperson with a distinct accent, a close-up of the package accompanied by a trumpet sound, a smile with an over-the-top glint and accompanying "ting" noise, the word "fabulous," and a consistent tagline: "For a good clean feeling, no matter what." That's a lot, but all of these elements worked in unison to help consumers recognize the brand and take away the intended message.

These different elements are important because they can be valuable markers that the creative team needs to be aware of. And understanding the importance of brand elements sets the discussion for our first pillar: personality.

Personality. As illustrated in the Orbit gum example, most established brands have a preferred means in which they like to represent their brand. Some clients even call this the personality of the brand, which should be reflected in brand communications. For us, personality reflects the specific way we represent our brand in our communications: lighthearted, somber, empathetic, funny, etc. For example, Canada Goose—known for their premium cold-weather coats—is often serious and professional in their email communications to consumers. In contrast, Bombas—a designer of ultra-comfortable and durable socks—sends emails that tend to be more lighthearted and humorous in nature.

Like people, brands can have varied and distinct personalities. Whether they channel the personality of a serious scientist or a witty aristocrat, successful brands have learned how to create communications with a similar voice and similar brand elements. As an example of a brand that often does this to near perfection, let's consider Nike. In our classes and workshops, we often show the first fifteen seconds of a Nike ad from another country, cutting it off before any conspicuous logo or known athlete appears. We ask students to identify the brand. Most students can, but then we ask how they knew. This is where it gets interesting. The music. The look on the athlete's face. The way the camera is shooting the action. These distinct pieces help reveal the brand personality and help consumers quickly identify the brand.

In some cases, the personality of a brand naturally emerges out of its offering. "Cards Against Humanity" is a popular and satirical card game whose marketers channel the humorous nature of the product into irreverent advertising. For example, previous promotions have included selling literally nothing for five dollars (they had fourteen thousand sales of nothing). One year they even asked consumers to help them dig a hole—consumers donated more than $100,000 to this initiative. The hole served no functional purpose as the FAQs clearly stated. Indeed, this seems like an inane waste of money; however, for a brand that thrives on being irreverent, it fit perfectly while generating both awareness and love from its consumers. In other cases, the personality of the brand is used to contrast it from competitors. Under Armour athletic wear is often serious and aggressive in its advertising, and this distinguishes it from other brands in the athletic wear category. Of note, companies identify (and codify) their personality based on current market perceptions, competitive brand personalities, and an ideal future state. Some firms even create a guide that outlines the brand personality for all agencies to consistently use. This codification is particularly important in social media or inbound content marketing where a brand might have several different people acting as "the voice." From the outside it should sound as one.

Just because a brand has a personality does not mean it cannot—or should not—adapt to the situation. Indeed, we all have personalities, but most of us behave differently at home, when on a date, or when at the workplace. In a similar fashion, a brand can adjust its tone or behavior for a particular situation. A number of factors affect the tone that is appropriate for a brand. A brand's Twitter response to a customer complaint is likely to be different than a more lighthearted response to a humorous story involving the brand. In other cases, contextual factors in the environment might shape the appropriateness of the tone in an advertisement. For example, amidst the COVID-19 outbreak, numerous brands launched ads with a more serious tone to align themselves with the current sentiment. In contrast, commercials aired during the Super Bowl have historically gravitated toward being upbeat and funny to capture the festive spirit of the event.

The key is to make sure, while adapting to the situation, you do not engage in actions or behaviors that create confusion around your brand personality. You may act differently in a meeting than at dinner with colleagues, but no one is questioning whether you were swapped out with a different person. Strong brands often have similar brand elements across situations, but they adjust the tone in a manner that fits the specific situation.

Mandatories. Mandatories are requirements placed on the creative team. These mandatories might reflect specific actions that must be performed in the execution. For example, across decades of advertising, Jif Peanut Butter required commercials to feature peanuts transforming into peanut butter as a means to illustrate the large quantity of peanuts in every jar. Google might require that any advertisement for the search engine show some search terms being typed into its browser. Mandatories are often used to reinforce or convey brand elements and brand personality.

When it comes to mandatories, we need to be judicious. This is not our place to try to take over the job of our creative partners; we have creative partners because they excel (or should) at bringing the brief to life in a powerful way. However, it is important that the creative team understands any must-haves in the final product.

Mandatories can also help the creative team understand potential legal matters and the importance of how a message might have to be phrased.

For example, in the supplements industry, brands have to be careful that they do not overpromise or convey the wrong message to consumers. A strategist should make this clear in the brief before the start of the creative work. Similarly, if corporate guidelines exist such as diverse casting requirements or policies regarding comparative advertising, this should also be addressed in the brief. Agencies, of course, prefer fewer guardrails, so you want to make sure any "mandatories" are truly mandatories. They also hate last-minute surprise changes, which is why it is better to include the mandatories in the brief.

Timing and Budget. When planning an ad, we generally have a rough idea of both when we want it to go live—timing—and how much money we want to spend creating it—budget. Timing and budget are important because the creative team uses this in-market date to back out a time line for creative development and production. Moreover, if testing for the campaign is desired, both testing and revision time can be built into the time line. Thus, timing involves understanding not only when the campaign will run and for how long but also the critical milestones prior to the launch.

Budgets can vary widely with the democratization of production technology and the varying media needs. A simple social media post can be done for next to nothing; a Super Bowl commercial can easily cost more than $1 million, and the media buy will likely be in excess of $5 million. Budget is also affected by whether you will test and how aggressively. Many firms have a historical context for the budgets they are willing to commit to production, often correlated to the amount of money that firm will spend on media to show the ad. As is often the case, you generally get what you pay for.

Media. Finally, you have to know where the communication is going to run. Is it a trade show or a TV spot? The agency needs an idea of what the likely media channels will be in order to properly plan and create the matching executions. For example, knowing the media channel(s) allows the agency to ask tactical questions such as "Does it need to be in portrait mode as well as landscape mode?"

If you are briefing a large campaign with multiple executions in multiple media channels, it's often advisable to ensure that the creative idea will work in different formats. We're long past the era of seeing a campaign in just television and print. In fact, you might even ask for some "sample" executions as part of the time line. While it is often not feasible to see every possible creative idea brought to life in every potential format, you can often specify two or three varying formats (e.g., fifteen-second video, podcast, in-store poster) just to see the potential range of a campaign. As you progress in development, ask to see the ideas presented in the context within which they will be displayed. What looked great on a poster in the conference room may not work when you see a mock-up on a seven-inch phone screen.

As discussed in Chapter 3, media planning also involves dividing your budget across different media channels to best achieve your communications goals for your target. Media planning is often done in conjunction with a media agency that works with your objectives, target audience, and budget to plan and buy the placements of your ads. Media planning involves a balance between three levers: **reach**, how many members of your target audience will see the ad; **frequency**, how many times an individual sees the ad in a given time period; and **continuity**, the sequencing of the media over a given time period. Brands work to optimize the "flighting" or timing of when they are "on" and "off" in order to achieve the best results at an efficient spend level. Media agencies specialize in determining the right reach and frequency for a given goal and then identifying the most appropriate channels and timing to reach the intended audience.

Value to Clients and Agencies

. . . .

Like a movie, creating an advertising campaign is often time- and resource-intensive. One of the key benefits of a well-written creative brief is to minimize swirl—needless back and forth between client and agency—that costs time and money. This concern is particularly true in the execution section of the brief, and minimizing swirl helps both the client and the agency. As has been said, the devil is in the details, and failure to note crucial details can derail the production process. Finding out late that the budget is not close to what's needed to produce the approved concept—not good. Learning that the core of the spot hinges on a line that the legal department will not allow—a deal breaker. A mention at the end that this sixty-second online video needs to be edited into something that makes sense in a five-second vertical format for social media—the train has left the station. Avoid the pain. Think through these issues now. This is what the execution section and the four pillars force us to do.

The establishment of consistent brand elements is also essential. As a client, you will likely oversee creative output from multiple sources inside the firm and from agencies. We've done something called the **one wall test**, where you put all the creative output on a wall (ads, posts, white papers/content, in-store materials, search engine language) and see if all the elements appear to come from the same source. Spoiler: they usually don't! Understanding the brand elements that drive brand recognition and attitudes helps the creative team understand how to build and reinforce your brand in the execution across channels.

Some aspects of the execution are particularly helpful in newer client-agency relationships. Explaining your brand personality helps the agency understand the tone and landscape for the advertisement. Is our brand whimsical or composed? Will this be intense or lighthearted? Are you aiming for the aspirational tone of Nike? Are you willing to push the boundaries and embrace irreverence like Cards Against Humanity? Conveying your brand personality helps the creative team develop your strategy in a tangible way that is comfortable and consistent with your brand.

Why Brands Fail and How to Succeed

Although the execution section of the creative brief is more tactical in nature, we have seen great strategies crumble because of poor direction when it came to the tactics. To us, successful brands tend to ask a few critical questions—and unsuccessful brand fail to ask these questions.

Where else might I use this? On the surface this is a simple question, but it has huge ramifications. We have seen brands develop an execution they are proud of. However, they developed it for a specific channel and local market and did not think through the various media outlets it would or could appear in. Brands forget that the execution might have international exposure and, while effective in some countries, it might be disastrous in others. Egregious examples exist of brands failing to consider how a given piece of creative will translate in a different market. The American Dairy Association's "Got Milk?" campaign was translated to "Are you lactating?" in Mexico. If you do not think about the various platforms you might use the ad on, you might get the perfect ad for a very limited set of use occasions. More commonly, brands take creative elements designed specifically for one format and try to apply them to another—perhaps a landscape-oriented online video squished into a social media portrait view—it doesn't work, and those are wasted media dollars.

Agencies aim to optimize the budget to produce the best deliverable for the given use. That means they are probably not negotiating with any actors for worldwide usage rights if you've never mentioned the ad might be used globally. It means that the ad could look terrible when squeezed down for social media. If you tell agencies ahead of time of the different possible uses, they can plan. Plan ahead for this discussion so you can be decisive. If not, all of a sudden you may find yourself asking things like "Why don't we just shoot it both ways to be safe?" That is a great way to have your budget balloon out of control.

Unrealistic or poorly managed time frames. Time lines often cause strife. Like with many projects, it would be better to have more time, but we're constrained by a delivery date. One of the first deliverables from the agency should be a time line for the ad campaign from development through production. When this time line is too long, unfortunately the first places to get cut are often brief development time and creative development time. By now, hopefully you realize that having a poorly thought-out brief will only cost more time down the road.

We have talked with clients who often complain or look to creative development time as a promising area for cuts. After all, does a creative team really need three to four weeks to come up with one idea? It depends. We've seen the best ideas come on the first day and conversely only come after weeks of trial, error, and debate. If the creative output is very import-ant to you, especially if you are doing something different than your last creative effort, be cautious in asking the agency to limit the time they say is needed to create the best results.

One sneaky place a time line becomes poorly managed and expanded is in approvals. The development process should include time for reviews, revisions, etc. We have seen this get out of hand. The first reason is that the number of creative reviews grows from two or three to five or six as the team is unable to decide on the best ad. It could certainly be an incompetent creative team, but more often this is the fault of a vague creative brief; the client and agency do not have shared guidance on what is actually "good."

The other area that causes the time line to get out of hand is lagging client approvals. Particularly in new relationships, we have seen clients underestimate the time needed to approve various elements along the process. Does the CEO also need to approve casting? Is she still even available given her other commitments? Take some time early on to understand the key approval points and who in the organization needs to approve them, and make those approvers aware now.

Mandatories that write the ad. Be very careful that "mandatories" are actually mandatory. This section can become bloated with the creative visions of multiple clients trying to shape the outcome. If you have a creative genius on staff, fire the agency and do it yourself. But chances are you don't. That's why you hired a specialist. Your job is the strategy. If you do it well, the creative team you hired can do their job well.

Minimizing nonworking versus working spend. In advertising lingo, "working" dollars are used to buy media and "nonworking" dollars are used to pay for research, agencies, and ad production. It's become popular recently for some firms to publicly decry the amount of money they spend on "nonworking" budgets in an effort to shift the dollars "where it matters"—showing the ad to people. Perhaps at first glance that makes sense. And we certainly would not advocate spending $3 million creating an ad that you will spend $1 million running.

The problem is that pulling support from "nonworking" investments assumes all ads are equal, and that is simply untrue. Such a perspective asserts the brand who finds a rich resonant insight has no advantage over the brand who doesn't. It assumes that great creatives and directors make the same ads as bad creatives and bad directors. It assumes that all creative briefs are equally good—they are not! A lot of assumptions exist that are not always true.

One exercise we like to do is to think through the ramifications via assumption-based modeling. That is, ask yourself questions about what would happen based on reasonable assumptions. What will the difference be if that ad is noticed 50 percent of the time versus 35 percent? How much would it matter if the main message is 20 percent more compelling because you found a richer insight to leverage? When you start to work through the impact of even a 5 percent improvement to creative output on a multi-million-dollar media buy, the investment starts to become more tangibly beneficial. And you can test it.

Revisiting the Brief

It's time to go back to our brief for Stark Cloud Solutions. Our original execution section read:

EXECUTION	Leverage Stark graphic assets. Primarily U.S. digital media.

We have noted the inclusion of some brand elements—"graphic assets." But we have not identified which graphic assets. Perhaps the Stark brand has a color palette, a spokesperson, a logo, a preferred company headquarters picture, etc. Are all the assets to be included? Are they all of equal importance? Then we have the media. Digital media can include everything from radio to outdoor to small social graphics, to videos ranging from three seconds to two hours. And the specific usage and the associated expectations of ads found within various social platforms differs considerably. Your Twitter ad is likely different than your LinkedIn ad; your YouTube ad is likely different than your TikTok ad. These are different media channels that require tailoring if you want them to perform effectively within the specific channel. And we're missing both personality and timing and budget. Put simply, even though we have some elements here, we've come up very short in the scheme of the execution section. Let's improve this with the following revision:

EXECUTION	• The brand personality is independent and self-reliant – see Stark brand book • Feature the Stark logo and consider use of "Stark blue" • Primary media focus: :08 Pre-roll video, business focused single image social media. U.S., Canada, Mexico • Campaign runs March-August with media budget of $3 million dollars and production/talent budget of $275k

Does that seem better? It should. Now, we start by articulating the brand personality. Two graphic elements are brought forth, the logo as mandatory and the "Stark Blue" to be considered. The primary intended media usage is identified, as is the potential need for two additional language translations: French for Canada and Spanish for Mexico. Finally, there is a clear budget and time line. With these simple additions, we have a much greater chance of limiting needless rounds of revisions and last-minute fixes. And while we have added some specificity, it has not come at the cost of keeping the brief concise.

Myths, Misconceptions, and Other Questions

"Rather than constrain the agency with a budget, isn't it better to just see what they come up with?"

Clients sometimes worry about sharing the budget with the agency. Part of this concern is that, if they reveal a number, the agency will seek to spend every last penny. Sounds like there might be some trust issues, but let's address this concern. You don't have to be exact, but you also don't want the agency coming back with $5 million ideas when you have $50,000. Nor do you want them to come back with a small idea when you have a $50 million budget for launching a new product! We strongly advocate giving a reasonable budget that you expect the team to meet, but then being open to arguments for increasing the budget if something warrants the extra money.

"Should I give the agency the media plan first, or should we wait for the creative idea to drive the media?"

We have seen agencies with very strong perspectives that the creative idea should drive the media. As they have told us, predetermined media plans can shortchange the potential of a great idea. There is some truth to this perspective, but there is also the danger of ignoring media all together. For example, you might have identified a media channel that allows you to reach your target in a cost-effective manner—if the channel is a powerful means to reach the target, then you want creative material that will play in that channel. If we know we can reach our targets on Instagram, we don't necessarily want the creative team to focus on a Super Bowl commercial.

Ultimately, we believe the answer to this question depends on the context. If your brief is for a campaign that you expect to live primarily in specific media platforms, then we think it's helpful for the creative team to have some guardrails as to the media outlets. In contrast, if you are not sure what media to play in, or you can choose to reach your target in one or more distinct channels, you might allow creatives to first generate the idea and then map it onto channels.

Remember, the creative brief is a road map. As creatives bring an idea to life, it is perfectly fine to revisit the media platforms under discussion. In the end, it is often about finding the balance of where we achieve the most from the creative idea, but also use media channels in an effective fashion.

"I saw the same ad four times in a row on the same show last night, and I'm annoyed by the repetition. Is that really on purpose?"

No, it's almost always a mistake, and if it was your brand, call the media agency. This question comes up routinely in our classes. Media frequency is important. Ads increase in effectiveness with repeated exposures along a curve that typically crests and then begins to decay. As mentioned earlier, the term we use for the decay section of the curve is "wear-out." At these frequency levels, the ad is producing less marginal benefit than earlier exposures. No simple rule for wear-out exists; it depends on a multitude of factors, including the complexity of the ad, the competitive context, the media format, and the customer targeted. But, for almost any ad, four times in a row would accelerate wear-out and probably cause negative associations, so it's to be avoided. What's interesting is that this phenomenon seems to happen the most in digital contexts where we have the ability to limit frequency with technology.

Measurement

. . . .

In 1628, after two years of construction, the Swedish warship *Vasa* set sail. Armed with sixty-four bronze cannons, the ship was to be the naval titan of its time. Unfortunately, the ship sank along with its crew before it had even sailed a mile of its maiden voyage. One explanation for the *Vasa's* sinking was an improper distribution of mass within the hull. How did this happen? When the ship was recovered from the depths in 1961, archeologists found rulers used by the shipbuilders. Two were calibrated in Swedish feet—twelve inches—but two were measured in Amsterdam feet—eleven inches. This has led people to suggest that the use of different measuring systems contributed to the improper distribution of mass that led to the *Vasa's* demise. Clearly, measurement is important.

Measurement plays an extraordinarily valuable role in advertising. First, just as proper measurement could have saved the *Vasa* from demise on its maiden voyage, proper measurement during advertising testing can prevent the disastrous failure of an advertisement in the market. Second, during or after a campaign has launched, measurement is crucial to understanding whether a campaign ultimately succeeded against its objectives. For these reasons, it is essential for managers to outline the measurement criteria that best map to the objectives; measurement allows us to learn when and why an ad succeeds or fails.

Unfortunately, in reality, clients and agencies often do not give measurement the weight it deserves. In our experience, clients even balk at testing when it is most needed. In other situations, measurement is not used to learn the truth about the performance of a campaign, but to make the brand manager or the agency look good. These are serious problems that can cause snowball effects where advertising dollars continue to be spent against ineffective efforts.

In recognition of this issue, our creative brief template embraces measurement. We make measurement an active part of the conversation *before* a campaign is undertaken. We do this to avoid the problems that come from poor measurement or a lack of measurement altogether.

Measurement: The Basics

Remember the importance of objectives covered in Chapter 2? Our measurement strategy should be in service of these objectives. If our objective is to raise awareness about a new offering, then we need measures that allow us to observe changes in awareness. In contrast, if our objective is to shift perceptions of our product's performance, then we want to assess changes in beliefs or attitudes. Indeed, if we design an ad campaign to change perceptions of quality, but all we measure is social media "likes," we may be measuring something that tells us nothing about the success of our ad campaign!

Clients and agencies can engage in measurement in a lot of ways. However, strong measurement focuses on the creative elements of the advertising and/or the combination of the creative elements and the media channels. In some cases, a portion of the measurement might take place before or near the beginning of launch to optimize our spend. In addition, a portion of our spend might be used after the launch to optimize market decisions or for future efforts.

As a primer, we discuss several common methods of measurement: focus groups, copy tests, market tests, and attribution modeling. Each of these provides different approaches in the service of understanding whether an advertisement execution might have the desired effects.

Focus groups involve talking with consumers to understand their response to an advertising concept. This might be the idea in a rough form—such as a storyboard, an animatic of the creative idea, or even the actual execution. We have heard people admonish focus groups for being unreliable and even outright useless. We view this as a myopic conclusion that likely stems from prior bad experiences or the improper use of focus groups. Sure, if improperly conducted, focus groups can reflect the qualities of unreliability and uselessness. However, used properly, focus groups can have tremendous value.

Here is an insight. One of the main problems with focus groups "not working" or "being useless" is they are used for purposes for which they are inappropriate. The qualitative research often provided in focus groups is meant to uncover what we did not know or did not think about. It's not a large sample, and the stimulus is often rough, so a focus group would not be helpful to "vote" on the best ad or even the ad likely to be most effective for a target. Rather, focus groups allow for a careful probing of reactions and thoughts to acquire potentially valuable information. Indeed, qualitative research from focus groups can sometimes reveal the "why" behind a success or failure in a quantitative test. Of course, focus groups have to be handled properly without bias by the moderator. If you lead consumers to give a desired response, then they may not offer a meaningful response to the creative; in fact, they may ultimately serve as little more than a "check box" to the process that might give the brand a false sense of confidence.

THIS AD IS DESIGNED TO APPEAL TO SMART, HANDSOME
PEOPLE. PLEASE RAISE YOUR HAND IF YOU LIKE IT.

When handled properly, focus groups can be a first line of defense on a number of fronts. If a focus group raises concerns that an ad might be insensitive with regard to issues of race, gender, or politics, this often suggests greater scrutiny of the creative is warranted. Likewise, if focus groups reveal unintended takeaways from the message—such as seeing your new chicken sandwich as unappetizing because you were trying to show it's so good it can be eaten even underwater—this suggests more probing may be needed. Alternatively, focus groups may reveal particular aspects of creative work that draw in the consumer; for example, a focus group may reveal that people find a particular spokesperson more interesting or attractive. A further advantage of focus groups is that a moderator can probe consumers' concerns to understand why a piece of creative material might not have the expected response. Indeed, when used properly, focus groups can be low-cost means to understand consumers' responses.

Copy tests can also be used to gauge creative output. Unlike focus groups that are often led by a moderator, copy tests can be done via surveys where people's beliefs and evaluations are measured before or after exposure to an ad campaign. For example, consumers might complete an initial survey that includes their perceptions of Starbucks. After seeing ads for the product, consumers might complete the measures a second time in order to assess to what extent the advertising shifted consumers' beliefs. One potential advantage of copy tests is that they often involve less leading of the consumers than can occur in focus groups.

People's responses following exposure to ad copy can also be compared to the responses of a group of participants who are not exposed to the ad copy. Again, brands can use these measures to understand whether the advertising produces shifts on dimensions of interest. Frequently the results are compared to past tests of the brand or category benchmarks provided by the testing firm. What dimensions should be evaluated? The dimensions of interest should be aligned with the objectives in the creative brief.

Traditionally, copy tests were done in a research setting within the context of viewers evaluating a new "television pilot" so as to best replicate a natural environment. This model allows for similar low-fidelity (unfinished mock-up ads) to be tested. Now these copy tests can be performed live if you have high-fidelity ads. For instance, leveraging platforms such as YouTube, an ad can be tested out in the wild among a small, controlled sample population. This new model has begun to blur the line between traditional copy tests and market tests. These are not full market tests since they tend to be smaller in scope; however, unlike traditional copy tests, they represent much more real market conditions.

Market tests involve testing an ad campaign either before "launch" with a small sample of the market (e.g., regionally or digitally) or as it is live in the market. Whereas focus groups and traditional copy tests tend to be removed from market conditions, market tests assess what the advertising does in the marketplace. For example, a brand might run two different versions of a Facebook ad to see which one gets more clicks and responses. Market tests can be valuable to gauge whether a campaign is successful (and ideally why or why not). Market test results can further be used to decide whether a campaign should remain in the market, be pulled, or be modified. We have worked with several brands that strategically shift their in-market spend to observe the causal change in sales as a function of how much advertising money is being spent. In doing so, these brands can establish an understanding of how changing the advertising dial affects sales.

Across these various approaches, we have another task: we have to make decisions about what to measure. As already noted, one common set of measures are the objectives we discussed in Chapter 2. Namely, we might measure people's awareness of what a product does, the favorability of their attitudes toward it, or their intended actions. As we have already noted, the objectives in our brief not only serve to help us understand what the advertising campaign should accomplish, but they can also direct us to what we should focus on measuring as well.

Another measure we like to use when possible are thought listings or thought protocols, sometimes called "verbatims." Thought listings involve asking consumers to report the thoughts that came to mind as they read, saw, or listened to an advertisement. These measures can be valuable because they can offer insight into why an ad led to a particular response on a more quantitative measure such as liking. If people only report liking or disliking an ad on a quantitative measure in a copy test, while helpful with regard to understanding efficacy, this measure does not tell us why people are positive or negative. In contrast, thought listings can help reveal the source of consumers' response. For example, we can learn if people like the ad because they love the brand position versus the celebrity featured in the ad. If they didn't like the ad, we can learn whether that was because they found it boring or offensive and what the source of that reaction was.

Attribution modeling consists of regression-based analyses in an effort to estimate the contribution of advertising to sales. The general idea is to use all potential variables we have available (ad spend, creative campaigns, channels, discounting, distribution changes, pricing, competitor actions, etc.) in a regression model to understand the impact on sales. Such models are often referred to as "marketing-mix" models or analyses. A proper marketing-mix analysis typically relies on years of input. In our experience, the problem with marketing-mix models is that they can be expensive and often rely on assumptions that make precise estimates a challenge. Indeed, a proper marketing-mix analysis is often a multiyear commitment with a brand that requires immense strategic planning.

Now in digital platforms, there is much excitement about the ability to track all of a customer's touch points prior to sale and then use those data for attribution modeling via regression. While it can be useful to see the various paths customers take to purchase, as well as to learn about the potential combinations of tactics that appear more productive, this approach is riddled with imperfections. Research suggests that these digital models vastly underestimate the impact of non-trackable interactions (existing brand equity, offline behaviors, etc.). We also find that the last step prior to online purchase is via Google Search. Here is the problem in a nutshell. Did Google Search make consumers buy, or was that just the door through which they always enter before purchasing online? This is not a recommendation to pull advertising from Google, just a warning to not blindly attribute credit for the sale. Put differently, even with multiple touch points and tracking of consumers, it can be a challenge to know the proper sequence of attribution or how much weight a given platform should receive in converting a sale.

Value to Clients and Agencies

We cannot overstate the value of measurement. For clients, measurement has several important implications. A sound measurement strategy helps link the results of an advertising campaign back to the objective. If the objective of our advertising campaign is to shift perceptions of the freshness of our orange juice, we want measures to assess how fresh people perceive our product to be. If we do not have such measures, we might find that an advertising campaign affected sales, but not for the intended reasons.

A cynical reader might be thinking, "Why does it matter how an advertisement increased sales—it increased sales!" Imagine that we ran a campaign with the goal of helping consumers realize that our cloud service offers superior security. The campaign was a "success" as evidenced by a 20 percent increase in sales. Let's further assume that, while sales increased, the campaign did not shift perceptions of security at all; it simply made people aware of our brand. Some might say that if we don't measure perceptions of "security" we are none the wiser, but it really does not matter. The problem is this: it does matter. The campaign failed to build equity around being strong in security. As a result, we cannot assume people understand this point of difference moving forward. Indeed, in order to attract additional users, we might have to double down on security or communicate it more effectively. Moreover, a savvy competitor might come in and steal share by claiming superior security. Thus, tremendous value exists in knowing why advertising increased sales.

The measurement strategy also has value to agencies in two forms. First, sharing the measurement strategy can help the agency better understand how their work will be evaluated. Second, new compensation models often involve the agency accepting some of the risk—but also more of the reward—for advertising. As such, when done properly, agencies benefit from measurement by having clear proof points of the effectiveness of their work.

Why Brands Fail and How to Succeed

. . . .

While proper measurement is a complicated subject, we can simplify it by focusing on two critical questions that clients need to ask themselves. First, do we want to spend resources—time and money—in test? Second, for both the test and the campaign, what will we measure? Brands succeed by knowing how to answer these questions (or fail because they do not). Let's examine each of these questions separately.

Deciding to test and what to test. The first question is, do we want to engage in testing? You might be guessing we will say, "Yes, we should always test." However, that's actually not true. Testing takes time and resources. At one extreme, think about what it would mean to test everything related to our communications. This means that each email, each comment to a consumer or customer post, and each variation of a billboard would require a separate test when going to market. That is not feasible. Even a brand that has a $100 million campaign across digital, television, print, and events would lack the resources to test every piece of content to its fullest.

If we can't test everything, what do we test? We see testing as holding particular value in specifiable circumstances. One particular set of circumstances that increases our propensity to test are those that involve **uncertainty**.

First, we engage in testing when we have different creative concepts that seem equally viable. That is, we have uncertainty about what idea should be produced. Consider a situation where we have a new stylish bomber jacket and we cannot decide whether we should go with a campaign that features a celebrity spokesperson—who has prestige and badge value—or an everyday consumer—who people might relate to better. Here we could do a test to gauge consumers' reactions and see whether the celebrity is worth the value to hire them. You might say, "But we could produce both and run both in the market, right?" We could, but that's more expensive than either option alone; if one ultimately better resonates with the consumer, we might spend more money to have a diluted message!

Second, we tend to engage in testing when we are launching a campaign idea. If we are launching a new brand or the complete re-envisioning of an existing brand, we might test aggressively since a brand-new idea often has significant uncertainty around it. Remember the maiden voyage of the *Vasa*? It would have been a great idea to double-check the measurements prior to that voyage! However, had the *Vasa* successfully completed its maiden voyage and sailed the seas for a few years, the crew would likely have become fairly calibrated to the ship's stability. Or, if there had been little change in cargo during a trip, the need for measurement might have been attenuated. Once you have a strong working concept, uncertainty is reduced and with that so is the value of the test. As another illustration, consider the iconic Absolut Vodka ads that always showed the bottle or its silhouette in some different context. The campaign had such amazing traction with consumers that the value of testing five years into the campaign is not the same as testing prior to its launch.

Third, we also put more emphasis on testing when there is uncertainty as to how the audience will respond. In particular, we are sensitive to content that may lead to a negative response from our audience. For example, if we have an execution that pushes the envelope on traditional gender roles, we might want to test whether our interpretation of the execution fits with how consumers see it. The last thing we would want is to try to communicate we are a progressive brand and consumers have a different takeaway. Or, if a broad audience beyond our target is likely to see our execution, we might want to be careful that we don't unintentionally offend important secondary targets.

The takeaway from this discussion is that uncertainty should shift you toward testing. This does not mean that if you are fairly certain, testing has no value. We could have a lot of certainty and still be wrong! Additional factors beyond uncertainty can drive testing. In high-stakes situations—such as a Super Bowl ad—a brand that is fairly certain about a creative concept might still test. The stakes are sufficiently high that they want to know the concept works even if everything indicates it should. Indeed, when investing a lot of money into an advertising campaign, testing might be used to be sure one is not blindsided. In the end, even raising the question of whether an idea merits testing is a big step forward for a lot of brands.

Not setting the measurement criteria up front. We need to point out one of the classic and most egregious errors we see in marketing: brands do not put together a measurement strategy until *after* a campaign runs. This is wrong in about as many ways as you can be wrong.

First, not having a measurement strategy in place prior to a campaign launch means we might not have good measurement practices in place when the campaign is run. If our goal is to change consumers' attitudes, but we don't measure their attitudes prior to the campaign launch, it may be difficult to know whether they have favorable attitudes toward the brand because of the advertising. Any attitudes we measure might result solely from consumers' experience with the product or word of mouth;

the advertising might have even pushed the wrong associations! However, because the measurement was not planned, no control or comparison group exists. Essentially, by not having a measurement strategy in advance we put ourselves in a position of disadvantage in measuring the effectiveness of the communication.

Second, the lack of a measurement strategy can lead to a confirmation bias whereby firms seek to demonstrate that the campaign worked. That is, they seek out any measures that look good. Sales are not up? How about our YouTube likes? No? Did we get earned media out of this campaign? And so on. Former students—much to their own dismay—have told us they were tasked with "proving" a campaign was successful after the fact. The problem here should be obvious. While we want our campaigns to succeed, we need to know when they fail. If we look for measures that make a campaign look good, we might continue to spend money on an ineffective campaign. Poor measurement can give us a false sense of confidence that leads us to invest more money in a failed direction. It is for this reason that we have "measurement" as a section in our creative brief. This forces us to put forth a test and measurement strategy before the campaign is executed. In doing so, we can avoid the pitfall of trying to change successful results and instead focus on truth. When we fail, we can acknowledge the failure and change course to succeed.

Not sharing your strategy with your agency. People sometimes believe that measurement strategies do not need to be shared with agencies since they are separate from the creative strategy. In contrast, we recommend sharing your measurement strategy. As we noted, sharing the strategy can help the agency align with regard to incentives. However, sharing a measurement approach early can allow the agency to offer guidance as to whether the approach is sensible. We once talked with an agency that found a serious flaw in a client's measurement strategy. The client wanted consumers' perceptions of a product's cleaning power to shift from 40 percent to 50 percent. The client came back to the agency and reported that perceptions shifted only to 44 percent. The agency asked to review the measurement strategy. As it turns out, the client had used a third party that measured cleaning power among male and female consumers. The problem was that the product, and thus the advertising, was marketed specifically toward female consumers. Among female consumers, the purchase intentions increased to almost 60 percent! Involving the agency can prevent such errors.

Revisiting the Brief

Our original measurement approach represented in the Stark brief was:

MEASUREMENT	Ad adheres to brief. Sales in Stark Cloud increase 5%

Now, it should be fairly obvious how this can be so much better. The execution adhering to the brief is the lowest bar. Having a defined goal like a percentage change in a measurable metric is also good. But let's improve it:

MEASUREMENT	• Copy test perceptions of Stark's data security advantage relative to internal storage pre vs. post ad exposure • Use in market experiments to evaluate shift in beliefs around secure data protection

We have not changed too much, but look at how much more meaningful this revised portion of the brief is. We've tied the measurement to the specific objective that we determined was most important to this effort—shifting perceptions. A prelaunch test is identified as well as in-market testing of the finished ad. A couple of simple changes have put us on the path to a much more rigorous measurement strategy. And, like many aspects of the brief, it is fine if we have another document that dives deeper into the measurement approach (e.g., the wording of our measures), but what we have here is sufficient for both us and the agency to understand what will be measured and when.

Myths, Misconceptions, and Other Questions

"I should measure everything."

We often hear people suggest that the answer to "what to measure" is simply to measure everything. We understand how this can be attractive—you do not want to miss anything. As we said earlier in this chapter, the problem is that we cannot measure everything. This is easy to illustrate. Think about everything we could measure when it comes to a digital ad. We could measure consumers' attitudes, we could measure their response to the color scheme, we could measure perceptions of all sorts. It becomes very easy to generate a list of questions that reveals measuring everything is simply impossible. Indeed, once you start listing everything that could be measured, the realization that measuring everything is infeasible sets in.

Moreover, the more we measure, the more we risk two potential problems. First, the more questions we ask in a survey, the more one response from the consumer might influence another response.

For example, we ask consumers whether a tissue is soft, and consumers say, "It's good." Then we ask whether the tissue is high in quality. They say, "Well, I just told you it was good, so, sure, it's good." That second response does not actually inform us on the perceived quality of the product; it is just another measure of the first response. To limit such "bleeding" of responses we have to narrow the number of questions we ask. Second, the more we measure, the more the client and the creative team tend to read into things they should not. For example, we might say, "Isn't it interesting that this ad did not affect perceptions of price?" Maybe. However, if it isn't central, it can take us down a deep rabbit hole.

"If I pay for testing, it ensures my ad campaign will be good."

We hear this one far too often. People assume that engaging in testing guarantees success. This train of thought presents at least two problems: imperfect stimuli and poor testing. What we mean by imperfect stimuli is that frequently we are testing ideas and concepts before they are fully formed ads. Maybe it's reading a script to a focus group or showing a cartoony animatic. These are our best attempts to simulate the end product early before the time and expense of finishing an ad. The ad can and often will be made significantly better in production, so much so that some agencies refuse to test ads in nonfinal form. The inverse is also true. What seemed to perform well in its simplest form grows into a convoluted mess as a finished product. This is not meant to scare you off from testing early—just go into it with open eyes.

The value of a test can be botched in many ways. If you lead consumers down a particular path, as illustrated in our comic earlier in this chapter, then they might tell you what you want to hear. However, their input does not mean that when consumers—who are unaware of your narrative—see the campaign in the market, they will have the same reaction. In one example, a car brand tested an ad for a commercial prior to airing it. They told consumers they wanted to convey how much they wanted to serve the consumer by using excerpts from a civil right leader's speech. After a moderator had walked them through the narrative, the consumers congratulated the brand and gushed about how much they liked the concept. However, when the execution aired, people did not have that narrative. They viewed the ad as an insensitive appropriation of a civil right leader's speech.

"I already produced my campaign, so it is too late to test."

This is a popular myth. It is never too late to test. Indeed, we know of brands that have lived and died by whether they believe this myth. Those that died believed the myth and went ahead and ran a campaign even though they were warned it had negative overtones—those ads did not go well, and people were fired. In hindsight, it is clear canceling the campaign or replacing it with existing content would have brought a much better outcome. Brands that have lived by disregarding this myth have pulled fully produced campaigns after realizing they would not work or they would represent their brand in a negative light.

"We can never offend anyone (is it possible to never offend anyone these days?)."

This is a question we are getting with more frequency as we see brands lambasted by various groups because of their ads. The answer is that you can certainly choose to offend certain people if you wish. If you are Nike and decide that a Colin Kaepernick ad is going to make your target love you more while you anger other segments, that's a strategic choice. What we don't want is for you to be called into the CEO's office to explain how you accidentally offended a huge population because you "just didn't catch it."

"Ad testing replaces strategic decision-making."

All research is an input into your decision-making as a manager. We must ensure our tests are designed well and carefully weigh the results in conjunction with our own judgment and knowledge. Relying only on testing can lead to bad outcomes too. Let us share an example. Orbit gum had a long-running campaign that propelled the brand to number one in the category and became arguably the most successful campaign in the company's history. However, the copy testing for the initial ad was terrible. The ad was tested as an "animatic"—a low-fidelity, almost cartoon of how the final ad would look. It was confusing. All it seemed to have going for it was that it was very different than anything else in the market. The brand director and the agency reviewed the results and talked through the changes that could be made to improve the spot. The results were not ignored, but they were not used in a deterministic fashion. They were weighed and then leveraged to create a very effective ad campaign.

Agency Relationships and Creative Feedback

STARK CLOUD CREATIVE BRIEF

OBJECTIVE	Increase perceptions that Stark Cloud has the most secure data protection" from 15% to 35%"
TARGET	SMBs from $50MM to $150MM in sales whose existing servers are reaching 5 years in age
INSIGHT	The target is frustrated by the costs and resources of internal storage. However, they accept these costs because they fear that cloud data storage is unsafe and will be compromised
POSITION	Stark Cloud is the data storage service (FOR) that is even safer than your internal storage (POD) because of its industry-leading encryption methods (RTB)
EXECUTION	• The brand personality is independent and self-reliant – see Stark brand book • Feature the Stark logo and consider use of "Stark blue" • Primary media focus: :08 Pre-roll video, business focused single image social media. U.S., Canada, Mexico • Campaign runs March-August with media budget of $3 million dollars and production/talent budget of $275k
MEASUREMENT	• Copy test perceptions of Stark's data security advantage relative to internal storage pre vs. post ad exposure • Use in market experiments to evaluate shift in beliefs around secure data protection

We have finalized our brief. Our work is done, right? You should know by now we like to use rhetorical questions. Of course we are not done. Now that we have a strong brief in hand, the process with our creative partner begins. For brands that work with an external agency, this means it is time to brief the creative team. For brands focused on internal teams, it is time to take the work to our creative colleagues. And for entrepreneurs who are both client and creative, well, it is time to take the road map and put it into action!

For the purpose of this chapter, and our Stark Cloud Solutions brief, let us assume that we are working with an external agency. Furthermore, after briefing our agency, they have had a month to put together an initial execution. Everyone gathers in the room with a couple of virtual onlookers and here's the first ad we see:

Stark Industries Did you know that Stark Cloud online service storage is even safer than your internal storage because of it's advanced methods?

What are your impressions of the ad? Is it good to go online? If you are like us, your train of thought might be something like the following.

You see the Stark blue (just pretend it's blue). You see the message; it does appear to reflect the brief. So far so good, but you kind of hate everything else about it. So you start in on the agency, trying to be delicate: "Listen, I appreciate the effort, but I don't think this ad works. This picture doesn't seem appropriate. The font is also hard to read. Honestly, it's a little disappointing that you aren't farther along after a month."

You're not wrong in your reaction; however, sharing it in this way has just led to a series of mistakes that will lead to more development time and an eroding relationship with the agency that benefits neither party. These are real problems.

Creative development can be messy. It involves humans, usually creative humans who often see the world differently than you and most certainly have had vastly different training and experiences than you. Not only that, but in creative development, you're often forced to review ideas in very early stages. They aren't completely finished. The polish and luster that are part of the final product have not been applied. Sometimes they are just ideas. But you have to give feedback, helpful feedback. You have to enable the creative as opposed to shutting them down. However, because the creative process is messy, evolving, and ultimately human, it causes problems.

In this chapter, we equip you to lean on your brief to have meaningful and productive conversations with your creative partner; the upshot is you can enhance the value of the exchanges and produce better outcomes for both parties.

Creative Feedback: The Basics

After we have briefed the creative team(s), they start ideating to develop concepts. Great creative teams often generate many ideas—a lot are bad and a few they like. The few they liked were mostly killed internally by their creative bosses or someone else. By the time they reach you, their precious ideas have been filtered like dirt through a sift and they believe what is left is gold. As a result, most creatives are generally excited about the ideas that have survived to be shared with you. Put differently, in many cases, you are not seeing their first attempt or effort—you aren't just seeing a random thought by the team, but something they have put substantial time into.

Now, before the meeting with the agency even starts, you have to meet with your own team on the client side and prepare. Plan with your team ahead of time as to how you want to deliver the feedback. The goal here is to make sure you are not tripping over each other or using the feedback session as a brainstorming session with little structure or form. One important question to answer is when feedback will be provided. Will you respond to the agency immediately or ask for a quick private meeting to consolidate your team's thoughts? There is not one right approach here. A lot depends on how you and your team prefer to operate. When working with new team members, it can be helpful to have a quick recess to debrief internally so you don't contradict yourself or provide conflicting ideas to the creative team. A second important question to answer is how feedback will be provided. Will the most senior person go first? Or might the more junior person go first so that the senior person can assess them? The answer might depend on your own team goals. We have seen different approaches meet with success, but the common element of success is to have a plan.

Now, let's turn to the meeting itself. In the room, the account person—the agency lead that manages the client-agency relationship—reads through the brief to ground everyone in the strategy. While this might seem procedural, it is actually a critical moment. Listen carefully to make sure their representation of the brief is true to the brief you delivered. When the brief has been delivered, a hush often descends upon the room, and the creatives start to present their ideas. The creatives will begin an engaged presentation because they are genuinely excited about the concepts they have. Importantly, what you will see is almost never the final execution. The earlier, the more rough it is. Yes, it would be more diagnostic to see the fully completed ad, but with more fidelity comes more time and money. Consequently, early in the approval process, we often see ideas in low-fidelity infancy: a script or storyboard outlines the key moments of an ad; placeholder imagery and rough copy might accompany a print or digital image. For some projects, a team may even create something that looks like a finished ad. Regardless of the fidelity, the goal of the creative team at this stage is to convey to the client the central idea of the ad based on the creative brief. Our job as strategists is to understand and visualize the finished output so that we can have a productive conversation and ultimately select the ad idea with the greatest likelihood of accomplishing our objectives.

Managing these conversations properly can be a learning process. Let's start with some tips about how to make them valuable to you and to your creative partner. First, try to listen through the ears of the target with attention to the insight you crafted in your brief. Don't be afraid to laugh or smile or show regular human emotion. Smiling is not a final approval. Ask to hear it again if you'd like. Ask clarifying questions. It's not a bad idea to take notes, especially if you want to solidify your thoughts the second time you are seeing it. A primary goal in the conversation is to understand the core idea. To help you navigate through this process, here are what we have found to be the most useful categories to capture and organize our thoughts before providing feedback:

Things I love. Start by thinking about what is working well. Perhaps they have demonstrated the insight perfectly, or perhaps they have made the brand unmistakable. Unless we have chosen a weak creative partner, there is usually some aspect of the ad that merits high praise. Sure, they might have missed the mark or aspects of the brief, but it might have been in an effort to think outside the box.

Things I like. A step down from the things we love are the things we like. These are typically aspects of the work that did not wow us per se, but they are on brief and sound. It is our way of recognizing and helping the creative understand the basics that we appreciate and want to see in the work. The reason we separate out "what we love" from "what we like" is that it also helps the creative team understand what we value at different levels.

Questions. There will almost always be areas where we have concerns about an execution meeting part of the brief or in the ability of the ad to perform successfully. Note these concerns so you can ask the creative team how they see the execution achieving these goals. Notice that we start with the assumption that they have not forgotten important elements, but simply that at this point you see an issue to discuss. In practice, sometimes they did forget or deprioritize an important element. But often, after further explanation, we find that it has been addressed in another manner. It is also fair game to take note of choices that you do not understand. For example, if you are not sure why the creative chose to use a theme song from the 1980s, it's something you will want to ask them about.

Red flags. Finally, we have what we term "red flags." These often consist of what appear to be major deviations from the brief. For example, if we think the insight has been forgotten or lost in the creative idea, this will be a major issue to discuss. Red flags also consist of violations of corporate policies or legal or ethical concerns. Finally, red flags include areas that could cause a negative response in our consumers such as misrepresenting the brand's opinion on topics such as sex, politics, race, etc.

Things I love ♡	Things I like ☺
Questions ?	Red Flags ⚑

Properly organizing our thoughts is only half of the process. It is important to offer feedback in the right way. In our own interactions with creative, we offer feedback in a very methodical manner that helps us make progress with the creative team. Moreover, we have found this approach builds trust and ultimately pushes the relationship toward reaching common objectives, which is what both parties want. Allow us to share our approach with you.

Lead with the positives. Start by thanking the creatives and pointing out the strengths of the work. This follows from your thoughts related to what you loved and liked about the work. Lead with this positive feedback. You might be thinking, "Okay, so this is just to be nice." Actually, no, this isn't just to be nice. Yes, focusing on the positives is a good gesture that makes it easy for the creatives to digest the concerns and situate them properly against what is working in the execution. However, the primary reason to lead with the positives is different. We lead with the positives to make sure that we keep and enhance what's already working well. Eventually, we will get to things we want to add or change. However, if we haven't made clear what is working great, then those things are in danger of being cut to accommodate any concerns we have.

Frame the negatives correctly. Once we have shared the positives, now we have to comment on the questions or concerns. For example, you may have seen something that you know legal will not permit. The creative team needs to know this. More frequently, you perceive that an idea or execution is missing an element that you value or the execution has features present that are not true to your brand. The key is to bring the concern to the table without dictating the solution to the creative. That is, you have to frame the negatives in terms of the concern but avoid the temptation of doing the job of the creative team. They won't like us attempting to do their job, and usually we aren't qualified to do it—that's why we hired them!

For example, imagine that we think an ad will fail to stand out in a crowded space; worse, it looks like a cheaper version of a competitor's ad. We could unleash on the creative and tell them, "This execution is bad. You need to change the color scheme, find better actors for the picture, make the text bolder, and add a puppy—because people love puppies." See what we just did there? We started to do their job. Do not dictate solutions. Instead present the negatives as questions for the creative team to answer. You might say, "One of our goals for the campaign is to break through the clutter of other cloud storage ads. What are your thoughts on how this imagery delivers against that goal?" or "I am a bit concerned that the choice of characters will be seen as stereotypical. Can you walk me through the logic?" If you state your comment as a goal to reach or a question to answer—rather than a mandate—it will be much easier for the creative team to understand why you want the change, and the solution that they come back with will often be better.

I THINK WE CAN STILL MAKE THE LOGO BIGGER!

Be Honest. If you need some time to think about the creative work, ask for it. If something seems to be rubbing you the wrong way but you don't know why, you can share that. This conversation should be positive, but nothing is gained by avoiding conflict. The last thing we want to do is hold back our concerns or questions. Again, if we ask our concerns in the form of questions, we make it much easier for the creative team to respond in a way that can either assuage our concerns or help them understand and figure out how to address them.

There is often a lot to discuss in a meeting with an agency. As the client, it is important that we are prepared to close the meeting with a recap and be clear and specific about the direction in which we want the concept to be developed. It's important to realize that communication pieces often require trade-offs. More emphasis on one thing will by default lead to less emphasis on other things. We need to be crystal clear about our priorities. Ambiguity will lead to unhappiness down the road.

Elevating Conversations with Creative: The ADPLAN Tool

In the end, our main goal is to have an ad execution that delivers the strategy in an effective way. The brief is our guidepost for the strategy. However, we have seen people struggle when the creative fits the brief but something about the execution is off. The Stark ad example at the beginning of this chapter is essentially on brief. We see the representation of the insight. We see the positioning of the brand. However, being on brief does not mean the advertisement is effective. An advertisement that is on brief could still fail to grab the target's attention in the marketplace. Or an ad that is on brief could capture their attention but fail to convey the positioning. Or maybe the ad captures attention and conveys the positioning, but the consumer ultimately hates it. These reflect tactical failures of strategy.

In our interactions with clients, we have found they often lack a vocabulary to clearly articulate tactical concerns to agencies. Indeed, it can sometimes be intimidating for an assistant brand manager to give feedback to a prominent agency like Wieden + Kennedy, Goodby Silverstein & Partners, or Droga5. Fortunately, we have a framework and a vocabulary we use to identify common pitfalls in tactical executions. We call this framework ADPLAN, and it produces six critical questions by which to review an execution and to judge its potential effectiveness and avoid pitfalls.

The ADPLAN Tool

Attention	Does the ad engage the audience?
Distinction	Is the execution unique in delivery?
Positioning	Appropriate category? Strong benefit?
Linkage	Will brand and benefit be remembered?
Amplification	Are thoughts of target favorable?
Net Equity	Does the ad fit with the brand heritage?

Each element of ADPLAN is an aspect of effective advertising, and you'll find that most ad or copy testing services map back to these elements. We have found this tool specifically helpful in creative development to turn a comment from "I don't like this ad" to "Do we feel this ad will be distinct versus the competitive ads in the category?" Let's go through each briefly.

Attention is where effective ads begin. Does the ad draw and maintain people's interest? People have to want to engage with an ad rather than looking down at their phone or clicking the skip button on YouTube. As Bill Bernbach, founder of DDB, said, "If no one notices your advertising, then everything else is academic." Nothing else on the list matters if no one ever pays attention to your ad. In ad testing, this measure is commonly referred to as breakthrough or ad identification/recognition.

Distinction is the next element we consider. Is the execution different, particularly from competition? Way back in 1933, psychologist Hedwig von Restorff showed that distinctiveness drives memorability. Distinct ads can facilitate attention as well as increase our memory of an ad. Some brands have such high distinction that the brand is recognizable within a second of the ad. For example, Apple ran a famous campaign that featured dancing silhouettes enjoying the iPod. Although the brand was typically not identified until the end of the ad, most people identified it as an Apple ad immediately.

Positioning is the third element we look for. It's no surprise we value positioning; it is part of our brief. The reason we include positioning in this framework is that it serves as an additional "safety check" that the work brings forth the benefit from the brief. Is the correct benefit communicated in the ad or has it been miscommunicated the humorous story of the ad? You spent a lot of time carefully identifying the positioning. Make sure the correct positioning comes through. You'll often see this measured in testing as the "main message takeaway."

Linkage is used to refer to whether both the brand and the benefit will be remembered. Linkage is frequently measured as brand recognition. We can't count the number of times someone has told us about this "great ad" they just saw, but they can't tell us what brand it was for. If no one remembers that the ad is for our brand, then it has little value to us. If customers misattribute the ad to a competitor, then we are spending money to build the competition! One of our tests for linkage is whether we can describe or explain the ad to someone without mentioning the brand—the easier it is to do this, the more we worry about linkage. Linkage also applies to the benefit—the positioning could be clear in the ad, but it might be forgotten if people are distracted by other ad elements such as an attractive spokesperson. An advertisement for Chobani might take the position of being better for you because it is natural. However, consumers might simply remember, "I saw the Chobani advertisement; it had a bear." They remember the brand, but they fail to link the benefit to the brand.

Amplification is a term used to capture consumers' response to the ad. That is, regardless of our intentions, consumers ultimately have their own reactions to the ad. Put succinctly, amplification reflects the idea that it is not what an advertisement says but what the consumer actually takes away both emotionally (how they feel) and cognitively (what they think). You could have a powerful position that ultimately leaves consumers with a negative reaction. For example, Quiznos, a sandwich chain, ran an advertisement that featured a man who dropped his sandwich on the floor. The man has to reach down and pry the sandwich from his dog, who has begun to gnaw at it. The man finally wrestles the sandwich free, stands up in triumph, and takes a bite. What is the ad trying to say? It's trying to say, "The sandwich is so good that you will fight to eat it even after it has fallen to the floor and been chewed on by a dog; yes, it's that good!" However, a number of consumers had a different reaction, they were disgusted!

Usually amplification is measured by a simpler term: "Liking." Some of the most frequent causes of negative amplification or liking are sensitive content: ads that, intentional or not, are viewed as sexist or racist, rely on negative emotions, or use controversial spokespeople. This is where homogenous teams can travel into dangerous territory. As a safeguard, seek diversity throughout your teams, your agency's teams, and your testing. Making a bold choice to take a controversial stand is different than accidentally alienating a population because you missed something.

Net equity refers to whether an ad fits with the brand's heritage. Your brand is like a cup full of the associations your audience has filled it with over time. Your choices in advertising help fill your cup with the right associations through consistency. Make sure you are reinforcing your key elements or making a strategic choice to move in a different direction. To illustrate, in a classic example of a brand protecting its equity, BMW touted how its super handling and performance also meant it was a safe vehicle. BMW did not simply say it was a safe vehicle because such a claim might undermine the equity they had developed around driving and performance. Instead, they reinforced their equity of being the ultimate driving machine and explained how this performance—specifically its ability to handle the road—provided an additional benefit of safety.

Value to Clients and Agencies

We've been a part of interventions where things have broken down between the client and the agency. Timing is shot, the work is lacking, and the teams on both sides are frustrated. Frequently it's a communication breakdown. A huge cause is an unclear strategy that leads to amorphous work and then to debates about the work with no aligned central strategic guidepost to ground the discussion. Hopefully by now we have made clear that a strong creative brief is a valuable asset to prevent such breakdowns.

Even when the strategy is in place, we run into problems with creative feedback. The client thinks the agency isn't listening. The agency thinks the client is asking for things that make the work worse. To avoid these issues, we have to start with the assumption that we all want the same thing. We both want great advertising. We both want the brand to succeed. We both want to avoid pitfalls. Giving feedback in the correct way helps avoid the work becoming personal and keeps the focus on the work being effective.

By combining the soft skills of delivering feedback with the specificity ADPLAN enables, we can achieve better results consistently. The agency feels valued, the client's needs are met, the ads are better, and the time line doesn't stretch on with draining rounds of creative development and review. To be clear, a lot of thought goes into managing a relationship. However, these are some stepping stones that can help you begin to pave the right path.

Why Brands Fail and How to Succeed

We have gone over tools and techniques. Constructive and clear feedback goes a long way. Trust is harder to teach. Great client and agency relationships have worked because of trust. In almost every situation where a truly great ad came to life, it came because the agency and client had a strong relationship built on trust. Great creative work breaks through on a new level, and it's often the result of strategic risk taking. Notice that we say "strategic risk taking." We are not suggesting forsaking strategy—that would be the antithesis of this entire book. Rather it is a balance between the discipline of a strong creative brief and the creative having enough freedom to make an ad that breaks through the clutter. This often requires sound strategy, clever creative, and trust between the client and agency.

How do you build trust? It starts with the relationship. When you hire an agency, you're hiring people. Hire the agency with the people you see eye to eye with; there has to be a shared vision for your efforts to succeed. Hire the people who share your passion for your brand. Hire the people who will disagree with you when disagreement is warranted. Sometimes these people cost 5 percent more. Or their pitch idea was your second favorite. Hire the right people; hire these people.

Great clients do more than just hire the right people; they build the relationship. They spend time with the agency and have discussions about what work they like and don't like, and why. Great clients talk about advertising related and unrelated to the brand. You want a relationship where the agency can say "you're wrong on this one" and you're open to hearing it.

Our advice is to be a great client. This recommendation is not the same as being a pushover client. A great client cares about the work and cares about the team. Send a nice note to the agency head when the creative team makes a special effort. Thank the team for their time and work. Here's a secret. Every agency has good clients and bad clients (except for a handful of really good agencies that fire bad clients; yes, those agencies exist). What makes a bad client? Bad clients have weak briefs that call for weak and indistinct work. They have vague strategies. They are combative and shift blame. And it's no secret within the agency who the good clients are and who the bad clients are. Over time, agency people rotate to other clients within the agency and the good agency people ask to be rotated to the good clients.

As agencies learn who the good and bad clients are, the entire agency world starts to learn who they are. And as you progress in your career, the agency world will probably learn if you individually are a good or bad client. If your agency team is always turning over and you can't keep the "good ones," or if you're trying to find a new agency and many say "they can't participate in the pitch," look inward. Are you a good client? You should be. It's good for business and good for your career.

Myths, Misconceptions, and Other Questions

"I'm a junior client and will have to go first in feedback. What should I say?"

In most situations, say less. The common mistake is that junior folks will try to cover every last detail and by the end of their soliloquy everyone is confused, and they certainly haven't made the desired impression. Your job is to productively add to the discussion and "move the ball forward." The next person will add more, and your leader will finish it up. Prioritize your most important comments. Stay away from the minutia of the ad—location, casting, product placement, individual pieces of dialogue. We'll get to that. Focus on the idea. Keep to the brief and ADPLAN territories. If you keep your comments brief and sharp, others in the room can always ask your opinion on the other issues—in fact, they probably will.

"Does ADPLAN eliminate the need to test?"

It doesn't. However, testing is impractical at all stages of creative development. ADPLAN is helpful because it adds a critical lens that elevates our conversation in an extremely efficient manner. It can inform testing because it can help us focus our tests on areas where we find remaining questions or ambiguity after discussion. However, it is possible that your assessment of how an ad performs against the ADPLAN framework does not match up with how consumers actually respond. We are not our customers and thus the temptation of judging an ad in terms of our preferences always lurks. Put differently, when used properly, ADPLAN helps you avoid unnecessary tests or direct your tests, but it does not prevent the need for tests. Rather, per our discussion in Chapter 7, we have to ask when to test.

"If I fire my agency and get a new one, my advertising will vastly improve."

This is a funny observation, but one we have both heard on far too many occasions. Another way to think of this is "The problem isn't me; it is my agency." Maybe. Certainly it could be. One thing to keep in mind is the old saying "there are frequently more differences within an agency than between them." Bringing on a new agency is expensive—you will often pay both for several months—and time-consuming. Start with the leadership of your current agency to see if you can solve the problems. And ensure that the problem isn't with you—if you have a bad strategy, then you'll have the same issue in seven months with a new agency. Think about trying new people within that agency.

NOTES

Epilogue

. . . .

"All of this has happened before, and
it will all happen again."

J. M. Barrie, *Peter Pan*

A s you read this book, new advertising technologies will have appeared. Novel advertising properties will have blossomed. Some will have faded. The world of marketing communications will continue to evolve. Indeed, if there was a certainty about advertising and communications, it might be captured in the following truism: the tactics that arise in advertising and communication will forever be a moving target.

If one accepts this truism, a natural corollary follows from it. Namely, generating a grand regression model or communication equation to predict success is a fool's errand. Such an equation would consist of a nearly infinite number of variables in a constant state of flux. A tactic that worked for one brand one year might fail for another brand the following year. However, the fact that the grand equation might be shifting does not mean there are no constants. The reason we wrote this book is that we firmly believe one constant exists within the communication equation: **strategy**. A methodical approach to developing a strategy will always be valuable in fostering success.

Examples of advertising date back thousands of years from seventh-century BCE Chinese songs to Egyptian papyrus posters to medieval town criers. They sought our attention. They aimed to convey a message. And we can assume some did it better than others! In the past century, we have witnessed a revolution of advertising from newspapers, to radio, to television, to an explosion of digital properties. As the number of places to advertise and the numbers of forms of advertising increases every year, remember the value of strategy stays constant. To us the most powerful and efficient means to capture strategy is through the **creative brief.**

Although you may encounter the creative brief in different forms and structures, we have highlighted six fundamental elements that comprise a strong brief: objective, target, insight, positioning, execution, and measurement. Each chapter of this book has been designed to both introduce and refine your skills in producing a creative brief based on these elements. Moreover, we have discussed how to interface with your creative team to bring out the most value for both parties. Of course, all of this takes times, and the more you practice and rehearse the tools and approach we have shared in this book, the more automatic they will become.

To close, as J. M. Barrie observed—and as others before him have observed—there is a cyclical nature to the world. The same is true of advertising. However, no matter what changes, the value of strategy is unassailable. By learning, internalizing, practicing, and mastering the strategies laid out in this book, you will be in position to succeed.

Final Notes

. . . .

We'd love to hear about your successes and your questions at our website creativebriefblueprint.com. Our hope is to keep the conversation going.
Good luck,
Kevin & Derek